THE
CELEBRITY
SEX LISTS
BOOK

Also available:
The Lists Book
The Celebrity Lists Book

THE CELEBRITY SEX LISTS BOOK

MITCHELL SYMONS

First published in in 1998 by
André Deutsch Ltd, 76 Dean Street, London WC1V 5HA
www.vci.co.uk

André Deutsch is a VCI plc company

A catalogue record for this title is available from the British Library

ISBN 0 233 99414 9

Printed in Great Britain by WBC, Bridgend

TABLE OF CONTENTS

Chapter 1 The Object of
My Affection 9

Chapter 2 To Have and Have Not 14

Chapter 3 Romantic Liaisons I 28

Chapter 4 Romantic Liaisons II 47

Chapter 5 Tying (and Untying)
the Knot 63

Chapter 6 Love Hurts 98

Chapter 7 Kinky Sex 107

Chapter 8 Each To Their Own 118

Chapter 9 Love for Sale 130

Chapter 10 Sex Polls 141
Afterthought 152
Select Bibliography 155

Acknowledgements

To Louise Dixon and Anna Kiernan who are as fabulously helpful as they are sexy.
Other people I would like to thank are Russell Ash, David Thomas, Rob Woolley and
especially Jeremy Beadle – sex gods all.

To Penny – the sexiest celebrity I know.

Chapter 1

The Object of My Affection

2 CELEBRITIES WHO HAD CHILDREN WITH THE CHILDREN'S NANNY

1. When Peter Jay, the BBC journalist was Britain's ambassador to the US in the late 1970s, his wife, Margaret, (Jim Callaghan's daughter) conducted an affair with Carl Bernstein (one of the two reporters who broke the Watergate affair). Meanwhile, he got their children's nanny pregnant.

2. Robin Williams. The brilliant comedian and actor left his first wife for Marsha, their son's nanny. Robin and Marsha then married and went on to have more children.

4 CELEBRITIES WHO HAD SEX WITH THEIR WIFE'S BEST FRIEND

1. Peter Sellers (when married to Ann Hayes)

2. Kelsey Grammer (when seeing Tammi Alexander, a Playboy model

3. Jan-Michael Vincent

4. Roald Dahl (left Patricia Neal, his wife of 30 years, for her best friend, Felicity 'Liccy' Crosland, whom he subsequently married)

10 CELEBRITIES WHO FELL IN LOVE WITH THEIR SPOUSE'S SIBLING

1. Stavros Niarchos

2. Charles Dickens

3. George Sanders (after divorcing Zsa Zsa Gabor he married her sister Magda)

4. Peter Rubens (did it the other way round – marrying the sister (Helena) of Suzanne (his former mistress))

5. Peter Bogdanovich (also did it the other way round – marrying the sister (Louise) of his murdered lover (Dorothy Stratton))

6. King Henry VIII (also did it the other way round – marrying the sister (Anne Boleyn) of his erstwhile lover (Mary))

7. Catherine of Aragon married King Henry VIII after her first husband, his elder brother, Prince Arthur, had died

8. Wolfgang Mozart

9. Sigmund Freud

10. Robert Southey

35 CELEBRITIES WHO HAVE HAD TO FACE PATERNITY SUITS

These have not necessarily been proved.

1. Captain Mark Phillips

2. Tom Jones

3. Bobby Brown

4. Imran Khan

5. Arnold Schwarzenegger

6. Chris Sutton

7. Eddie Murphy

8. Diego Maradona

9. Robert De Niro

10. Mick Jagger

11. Mo Johnston

12. Yves Montand

13. Bjorn Borg

14. Charlie Chaplin

15. Ellery Hanley

16. Herbert Von Karajan

17. Julio Iglesias

18. Nicolas Cage

19. Roscoe Tanner

20. Sylvester Stallone

21. Dave Berry (not only was he not responsible, he wasn't even the man who'd had sex with the woman in the first place: it was some other man pretending to be Dave Berry)

22. Charlie Chaplin

23. Michael Jackson

24. Marlon Brando

25. William Hurt

26. John Wayne Bobbitt

27. Boy George (obviously thrown out – not least because, as George himself explained, he's never had full sex with a woman!)

28. Reginald Bosanquet

29. Prince Albert of Monaco

30. Billy Idol

31. Eric Clapton

32. Jim Morrison

33. Engelbert Humperdinck

34. Buster Bloodvessel

35. John Daly

5 CELEBRITIES WHO HAD A FATHER FIXATION

1. Sylvia Plath
2. Charlotte Brontë
3. Megan Lloyd George
4. Anna Freud
5. Gloria Vanderbilt

31 CELEBRITIES WHO HAD A MOTHER FIXATION

1. James Cagney
2. Sir Thomas Lipton
3. Adolf Hitler
4. D.H. Lawrence
5. Marcel Proust
6. Liberace
7. Oedipus (actually slept with his mother – by accident)
8. Gustav Mahler
9. J.M. Barrie
10. Johannes Brahms
11. Sigmund Freud
12. Elvis Presley
13. Guy de Maupassant
14. J. Edgar Hoover
15. Yukio Mishima
16. Stendhal
17. August Strindberg
18. Peter Tchaikovsky
19. Havelock Ellis
20. Paul Verlaine
21. Bill Tilden
22. James Whistler
23. Nero (actually slept with his mother – on purpose)
24. Harry Houdini
25. Frank Lloyd Wright
26. Andrew Carnegie
27. Gustave Flaubert
28. Clifton Webb
29. Sir Isaac Newton
30. Charles Baudelaire
31. Clara Bow

15 CELEBRITy WOMEN WHO HAD CHILDREN AFTER THE AGE OF 40

1. Priscilla Presley
2. Goldie Hawn
3. Esther Rantzen
4. Elkie Brooks
5. Britt Ekland
6. Lucille Ball
7. Jan Leeming
8. Audrey Hepburn
9. Gloria Vanderbilt
10. Ursula Andress
11. Elizabeth Barrett Browning
12. Claudia Cardinale
13. Patricia Hodge
14. Rosalynn Carter
15. Phyllis Logan

13 CELEBRITIES WHO BECAME ELDERLY FATHERS

1. Anthony Quinn (78)
2. Charlie Chaplin (73)
3. Clint Eastwood (67)
4. John Mortimer (61)
5. Andres Segovia (76)
6. Cary Grant (62)
7. Yves Montand (67)
8. Bruce Forsyth (58)
9. Marlon Brando (65)
10. Clark Gable (61)
11. Pablo Picasso (62)
12. Arthur English (61)
13. Francisco de Goya (68)

6 MARRIED CELEBRITY WOMEN WHO HAD CHILDREN WITH MEN WHO WEREN'T THEIR HUSBANDS

1. Katherine Mansfield
2. Dorothy Macmillan (Lord Boothby was the father)
3. Paula Yates's mum (Heller Thornton-Bosment was the mother and Hughie Green the father)
4. Lillie Langtry
5. Lady Emma Hamilton (Horatio, Lord Nelson was the father)
6. Dora Russell

5 CELEBRITIES WHO HAVE ONLY EVER HAD SEX WITH ONE PARTNER

(Other people in this book might have only had sex with one partner but these were the only ones I could find documented)

1. Jonathan Edwards (wife)

2. Cilla Black (husband)

3. Anita Harris (husband)

4. Jim Bowen (wife)

5. Barry McGuigan (wife)

1 CELEBRITY WHO HAD THREE DAUGHTERS BORN OUT OF WEDLOCK BY THREE DIFFERENT WOMEN AND NAMED EACH CHILD ELIZABETH

1. Robert Burns

4 CELEBRITIES WHO DID STRANGE THINGS TO THEIR PUBIC HAIR

1. Mary Quant. Her husband cut it into a heart shape

2. Jean Harlow. She dyed it platinum blonde and actually died of peroxide poisoning as a result of doing so

3. Paula Yates. She dyed it pink

4. Lady Caroline Lamb. When she fell in love with Lord Byron she sent him some of her pubic hair

Chapter 2

To Have and Have Not

━━ ━━ ━━ ━━ ━━ ━━ ━━ ━━ ━━ ━━ ━━

13 CELEBRITIES WHO DIED VIRGINS

1. Immanuel Kant
2. Sir J.M. Barrie
3. Nikolai Gogol
4. Queen Elizabeth I (she wasn't called the Virgin Queen for nothing)
5. Michael Collins (notwithstanding the fact that he was played by Liam Neeson in the eponymous film)
6. Elsa Maxwell
7. George Moore (though it was suspected that he was the natural father of Nancy Cunard)
8. Sir Isaac Newton
9. Anton Bruckner (despite his fixations with teenage girls)
10. Alfred Munnings
11. Alma Cogan
12. Hans Christian Andersen (was actually bisexual although he didn't 'do it' with either sex)
13. Edith Sitwell

20 CELEBRITIES WHO WERE SEXUALLY ACTIVE PAST THE AGE OF 70

1. H. G. Wells
2. Duke of Wellington
3. Mao Tse-Tung
4. Charlie Chaplin
5. Bertrand Russell
6. Victor Hugo
7. Brigham Young
8. Benjamin Franklin
9. Pablo Picasso
10. Francisco de Goya
11. Leopold Stokowski
12. Havelock Ellis
13. Johann Von Goethe (proposed to a 19-year old when he was in his 70s)
14. Anthony Quinn
15. Colette
16. Leo Tolstoy
17. Sarah Bernhardt
18. W. Somerset Maugham
19. Franz Liszt
20. King Louis XIV

215 CELEBRITIES AND THE AGE AT WHICH THEY LOST THEIR VIRGINITY

1. River Phoenix (4 – his family were members of the Children of God cult which encouraged adults and children to experiment with "God's gift of sex")

2. Richard Pryor (5 – seduced by a girl aged 7)

3. Terence Trent D'Arby (8 – ". . . it happened with a neighbour's daughter under my grandmother's house")

4. Joseph Cotten (8)

5. Sean Connery (8)

6. Federico Fellini (8½ – hence the title of the film)

7. Lord Byron (9)

8. Rossano Brazzi (10)

9 Casanova (11)

10. Howard Antony (11)

11. Jon Peters (11)

12. Harold Robbins (11)

13. Shane Richie (12)

14. Mick Jagger (12 – according to some reports. According to others, his first time was with a nurse, in a hospital where he was working during the holidays)

15. Simon Bolivar (12 – with his cousin)

16. Jimi Hendrix (12)

17. Billie Holiday (12 – the first time she *voluntarily* had sex)

18. Charlie Drake (12 – in a wood shed in the East End)

19. Don Johnson (12)

20. Paul McGann (12)

21. Johnny Depp (13)

22. James Caan (13)

23. George Michael (13 – heterosexual sex)

24. Gillian Anderson (13)

25. Curt Smith (13)

26. Mae West (13)

27. Bob Geldof (13)

28. Peter Andre (13)

29. Jon Bon Jovi (13)

30. Anton Chekhov (13)

31. Lennie Bennett (13)

32. Justin Hayward (13)

33. Trevor Sorbie (14)

34. Dennis Waterman (14 – ". . . to an older woman")

35. Clint Eastwood (14 – with a "friendly neighbour")

36. David Duchovny (14)

37. Emma Ridley (14)

38. David Chokachi (14)

39. James Joyce (14)

40. Cher (14)

41. David Niven (14)

42. Larry Adler (14)

43. Nick Berry (14)

44. Phil Collins (14 – in an allotment)

45. Phillip Schofield (14)

46. Derek Jameson (14)

47. Bruce Willis (14)

48. Kate Moss (14)

49. Natalie Wood (14)

50. John Barrymore (15 – with his stepmother)

51. King Charles II (15)

52. Shelley Winters (15)

53. Stephen Fry (15 – with a girl named Shelagh whilst listening to *American Pie)*

54. Bjork (15)

55. Peter O'Toole (15)

56. Art Buchwald (15)

57. Bobby Davro (15)

58. Burt Reynolds (15)

59. Jerry Hall (15) – to a rodeo rider who kept his boots on

60. Tina Turner (15)

61. Jack London (15 – with a girl who "came with" a boat he bought)

62. Uri Geller (15)

63. Sophie Anderton (15)

64. Angela Griffin (15)

65. Paul Ross (15)

66. Jenny Eclair (15 – the boy had done it to win a £15 bet)

67. Charlie Sheen (15)

68. Dustin Hoffman (15 – with a girl who thought he was his older brother)

69. Sara Cox (15 – in a field full of sheep)

70. Madonna (15 – in the back of a Cadillac)

71. Sting (15)

72. Tony Mortimer (15)

73. Damon Albarn (15)

74. Mike Stock (15)

75. Lynne Perrie (15)

76. Sally Field (15)

77. Jo Brand (15)

78. Georgina Hale (16)

79. Anthony Van Laast (16)

80. Darren Day (16 – in Tesco's car park)

81. Benito Mussolini (16)

82. Grigori Rasputin (16)

83. Leo Tolstoy (16)

84. Jean Harlow (16)

85. Claire King (16 – in the back of a Mini)

86. Dorothy Squires (16)

87. Brigitte Bardot (16)

88. Samantha Janus (16)

89. Camilla Power (16)

90. Rhodri Williams (16)

91. Mel C (16)

92. Chris De Burgh (16)

93. Richard Harris (16)

94. Dean Gaffney (16)

95. Teri Hatcher (16)

96. Dani Behr (16)

97. Raquel Welch (16)

98. Shirley Maclaine (16)

99. Ursula Andress (16)

100. David Baddiel (16)

101. Robert Burns (16)

102. Simon Gregson (16)

103. Sean Maguire (16)

104. Shelley Duvall (16)

105. Groucho Marx (16)

106. Barbara Hutton (16)

107. Jayne Mansfield (16)

108. Mary Martin (16)

109. Mike Tyson (16)

110. Ginger Rogers (17)

111. John F. Kennedy (17)

112. Barry Newman (17)

113. Corbin Bernsen (17 – the night that Bobby Kennedy was assassinated, just yards away)

114. Frank Skinner (17)

115. Lee Evans (17 – with the woman who became his wife)

116. Alexander Dumas Senior (17)

117. Steven Spielberg (17)

118. Cyndi Lauper (17)

119. Michelle Collins (17)

120. Keith Chegwin (17)

121. Joan Collins (17)

122. Erica Jong (17)

123. Carrie Fisher (17)

124. Dyan Cannon (17)

125. Betty Boo (17)

126. Mary Astor (17)

127. Chris Evans (17)

128. Samantha Fox (17)

129. Bel Mooney (17)

130. Victoria Adams (17)

131. Alicia Silverstone (17)

132. Bernard Manning (17)

133. Donna D'Errico (17)

134. Tina Hobley (17)

135. Julie Burchill (17)

136. Mark Lamarr (17)

137. John Leslie (17 – at a fancy dress party with a girl wearing a wedding dress with L-plates attached)

138. Ronnie Biggs (17)

139. Cathy Shipton (17)

140. Liz Kershaw (17)

141. Errol Brown (17)

142. Dr Ruth Westheimer (17)

143. Shaw Taylor ($17^3/_4$)

144. Charles Baudelaire (18 – on which occasion he contracted the venereal disease which would kill him 27 years later)

145. Walt Disney (18 – on his birthday)

146. Matt Goss (18)

147. Barbra Streisand (18)

148. Baroness Issy Van Randwyck (18)

149. Brian Glover (18)

150. George Layton (18)

151. Jancis Robinson (18)

152. Patti Boulaye (18)

153. Brad Pitt (18)

154. Harry Enfield (18)

155. Dai Llewellyn (18)

156. Harry Thompson (18)

157. Irma Kurtz (18)

THE CELEBRITY SEX LISTS BOOK

17

158. Zoë Ball (18)

159. Peter Stringfellow (18)

160. Jamie Lee Curtis (18)

161. Napoleon Bonaparte (18)

162. Brooke Shields (18)

163. Victoria Principal (18)

164. Margi Clarke (18)

165. Daniella Westbrook (18)

166. Sir Cliff Richard (18 – with Carol Harris, the wife of Jet Harris of The Shadows)

167. Lord Jeffrey Archer (18 – in a wood)

168. Vivien Leigh (18)

169. Tony Robinson (18 – with the woman who became his wife)

170. Erin Pizzey (18)

171. Susan Hayward (18)

172. Emma Noble (18)

173. Lillian Hellman (19)

174. Gerald Kingsland (19)

175. Pattie Coldwell (19)

176. Dr Fox (19)

177. King Edward VII (19)

178. Marlon Brando (19 – with an older Colombian woman)

179. Chris Tarrant (19 – "on a riverbank somewhere but I don't remember who it was with")

180. Alison Steadman (19)

181. Leslie Thomas (19)

182. Carol Drinkwater (19)

183. Mira Sorvino (20)

184. Victor Hugo (20)

185. Mary Wesley (20)

186. Gillian Taylforth (20 – ". . . at the vital moment he called me Brenda")

187. Joan Rivers (20)

188. Jackie Onassis (20)

189. Queen Victoria (21)

190. Jonathan Ross (21)

191. Yazz (21)

192. Dudley Moore (22)

193. Edvard Munch (22)

194. The Duke of Windsor (22)

195. Libby Holman (22)

196. H.G. Wells (22)

197. John Peel (22)

198. Debbie Reynolds (23)

199. Esther Rantzen (23)

200. D. H. Lawrence (23)

201. Elliot Gould (23)

202. Catherine The Great (23)

203. Hugh Hefner (23)

204. John Cleese (24)

205. Isadora Duncan (25)

206. Bette Davis (26)

207. Nesta Wyn Ellis (26)

208. Anita Harris (27)

209. Sir Alfred Hitchcock (27)

210. William Gladstone (29)

211. George Bernard Shaw (29)

212. Mark Twain (34)

213. Johann Von Goethe (39)

214. Marie Stopes (40)

215. Havelock Ellis (60 – the first time he was ever able to achieve vaginal penetration)

12 CELEBRITIES WHO ARE CELIBATE

1. Bruce Oldfield
2. Sir Cliff Richard
3. Alan Bennett
4. Liz Hodgkinson
5. Ann Widdecombe
6. Sinitta
7. Quentin Crisp
8. Margarita Pracatan
9. Bill Maynard
10. Jean Alexander
11. Alan Freeman
12. Irma Kurtz

Note:

Sir Alfred Hitchcock was celibate from the age of 42 which, considering that he only lost his virginity at the age of 27, didn't give him much of a sex life.

In September 1997, Edwina Currie admitted to not having had sex for three years.

In June 1997, Spice Girl Mel C declared that she hadn't had sex for more than a year.

28 CELEBRITIES WHO HAD THEIR BREASTS ENLARGED

1. Brigitte Nielsen
2. Jane Fonda
3. Shannen Doherty
4. Melanie Griffith
5. Iman
6. Morgan Fairchild
7. Melinda Messenger
8. Paula Yates
9. Farrah Fawcett
10. Pamela Anderson
11. Demi Moore
12. Dannii Minogue
13. Gena Lee Nolin
14. Courtney Love – she later had her implants removed
15. Scorpio (Nikki Diamond)
16. Rhona Nitra
17. Jane Seymour
18. Nicole Eggert (she later had her breasts reduced)
19. Tori Spelling
20. Loni Anderson
21. Heather Locklear
22. Anna Nicole Smith
23. Denice Lewis
24. Alana Hamilton
25. Mariel Hemingway
26. Cher
27. Tanya Roberts
28. Daniella Westbrook

2 CELEBRITIES WHOSE PENISES WERE PRESERVED AFTER THEIR DEATHS

1. Napoleon Bonaparte (it was eventually sold for auction where it fetched £2,500).

2. Grigori Rasputin (according to the Mad Monk's biographer, when he saw it 'lit looked like a blackened overripe banana, about a foot long ...").

5 CELEBRITIES WHO DIDN'T WEAR UNDERWEAR

1. Marilyn Monroe

2. Jayne Mansfield

3. Lady Emma Hamilton

4. Mamie Van Doren

5. Tallulah Bankhead

46 CELEBRITIES WHO ARE/WERE APPARENTLY 'WELL-ENDOWED'

1. Gary Cooper
2. Jack Nicholson
3. Ryan Giggs
4. Aristotle Onassis ('The secret of my success')
5. Carlos Leon (the father of Madonna's baby is nicknamed "Carlos the Tackle".
6. Robert Redford
7. Jack London
8. Matt Dillon
9. David Mellor
10. Adam Clayton (according to Bono)
11. Frank Sinatra (according to ex-wife Ava Gardner, "there's only ten pounds of Frank but there's one hundred and ten pounds of cock")
12. Dolph Lundgren
13. Liam Neeson
14. John Derek
15. Jonathan Ross (according to him, according to his wife)
16. King Charles II
17. Steve Wyatt (according to Madame Vasso according to Fergie)
18. David Duchovny
19. Henri de Toulouse-Lautrec (not just big in relation to his size but BIG anyway – he likened himself to a "coffee-pot with a big spout")
20. Bob Geldof
21. Errol Flynn (his party piece was to get it out and try to play *You Are My Sunshine* on the piano)
22. Grigori Rasputin (said to be thirteen inches long)
23. Jimi Hendrix (said to be as big as his guitar)
24. Charlie Chaplin ("the eighth wonder of the world" – at least according to him)
25. Humphrey Bogart
26. James Woods
27. Aldo Ray
28. Warren Beatty
29. Arnold Schwarzenegger
30. Richie Sambora
31. Marlon Brando
32. Steve McFadden
33. Babe Ruth
34. Sean Penn
35. Milton Berle (the comedian once won a bet when he was challenged by a well-hung man. Berle, however, only pulled out enough of his "manhood" to win the bet and no more)
36. James Hewitt
37. Kevin Costner
38. John Dillinger
39. Tom Jones
40. O. J. Simpson
41. Lord Byron
42. Tommy Lee (nicknamed "T" Bone)
43. Guy de Maupassant
44. Chico Marx
45. Franchot Tone
46. Joe DiMaggio

12 CELEBRITIES WHO ARE/WERE APPARENTLY *NOT* 'WELL-ENDOWED'

1. Howard Stern (by his own admission)

2. Frederic Chopin

3. Hugh Grant (according to him)

4. King Farouk I

5. King Edward VIII ("THE smallest pecker I have ever seen" according to one friend)

6. Napoleon (just one inch when he died)

7. Ernest Hemingway ("the size of .33 shell")

8. Johnny Bryan (according to ex-lover Amanda Dunn)

9. Cary Grant (according to ex-lover Maureen Donaldson)

10. F. Scott Fitzgerald (he compared his to Hemingway's and decided that they were both somewhat lacking in the todger stakes)

11. Vaslav Nijinsky

12. Rainer Maria Rilke

44 CELEBRITIES WHO HAVE HAD MORE THAN 1,000 LOVERS IN THEIR LIFETIME

1. Grigori Rasputin
2. King Ibn Saud (three women a night – except during battles – from age 11 until his death at the age of 72)
3. Sarah Bernhardt
4. Cleopatra (on one evening alone, she was repeated to have given blow jobs to 100 Roman soldiers)
5. Jimi Hendrix
6. Frank Harris
7. Hugh Hefner
8. Henri de Toulouse-Lautrec
9. Catherine the Great
10. Clara Bow
11. Pablo Picasso
12. King Solomon
13. Casanova (though modern revisionists now claim that the figure is under 200 – which would put the world's greatest lover on a par with a bond-trader from Chigwell)
14. John Barrymore
15. Bill Wyman
16. James Boswell
17. Julio Iglesias (about 3,000)
18. Lord Byron
19. Charlie Chaplin
20. Alexander Dumas Senior
21. King Edward VII
22. Duke Ellington
23. Errol Flynn
24. Paul Gauguin
25. Georges Simenon (he claimed the total figure was ten thousand)
26. Howard Hughes
27. Victor Hugo
28. John F. Kennedy
29. Franz Liszt
30. King Louis XIV
31. Aristotle Onassis
32. Edith Piaf
33. Peter Stringfellow (claims 2,000)
34. Elvis Presley
35. Napoleon Bonaparte
36. Herman 'Babe' Ruth
37. Marquis de Sade
38. Leopold Stokowski
39. Hughie Green
40. King Farouk I (he tried to have sex with some 5,000 women but regular bouts of impotence meant that he wasn't always successful)
41. Guy de Maupassant
42. Mick Jagger
43. Lola Montez
44. Mae West

14 CELEBRITIES WHO WERE RENOWNED FOR BEING 'BAD AT IT'

1. King Farouk I
2. Henry Fonda (according to ex-wife Margaret Sullavan)
3. Howard Hughes
4. Fidel Castro (has been known to smoke, read and keep his boots on during sex)
5. King Edward VIII (apparently, size *does* count)
6. F. Scott Fitzgerald
7. Groucho Marx ("I'm a very bad lay")
8. Jean Jacques Rousseau
9. George Gershwin
10. The Duke of Wellington (the Iron Duke – not the present one!)
11. Ernest Hemingway
12. Clark Gable
13. Benito Mussolini
14. John F. Kennedy

22 CELEBRITIES WHO ARE/WERE RENOWNED FOR BEING 'GOOD AT IT'

1. Errol Flynn
2. Mel Gibson
3. Charlie Chaplin
4. George Best
5. Alexander Dumas Senior
6. Mick Jagger
7. Gary Cooper
8. Leonardo DiCaprio
9. Victor Hugo
10. King Louis XIV
11. Sylvester Stallone
12. Pablo Picasso
13. James Boswell
14. Grigori Rasputin
15. Jimi Hendrix
16. John Barrymore
17. Honoré de Balzac
18. Jack Nicholson
19. Joe DiMaggio
20. Babe Ruth
21. Guy de Maupassant
22. King Edward VII

5 CELEBRITIES WHO HAVE/HAD A LOW SEX DRIVE

1. Frederic Chopin

2. Sir Edward Heath

3. Cynthia Payne (famously preferring a nice cup of tea)

4. Damon Albarn (girlfriend Justine Frischmann said of him, "He has the lowest sex-drive of any man I've ever met")

5. Calvin Coolidge

8 CELEBRITIES WHO ARE/WERE PRODIGIOUS MASTURBATORS

Most men are keen on the old "five-finger shuffle" – after all, as Woody Allen says, "It's sex with someone you love" – but very few people are prepared to admit it. So good on you, Howard.

1. Howard Stern

2. Vaslav Nijinsky

3. Hans Christian Andersen

4. Andre Gide. He was expelled from one school for wanking in class

5. Yukio Mishima

6. Friedrich Nietzsche

7. Samuel Pepys

8. Jean Genet

10 CELEBRITIES WHO WEAR/HAVE WORN WONDERBRAS

1. Sharon Stone
2. Pamela Anderson Lee
3. Rene Russo
4. Geena Davis
5. Joanna Lumley
6. Mariella Frostrup
7. Kylie Minogue
8. Amanda De Cadenet
9. Jamie Lee Curtis
10. Heather Locklear

14 CELEBRITIES WHO HAD HRT (HORMONE REPLACEMENT THERAPY)

1. Kate O'Mara
2. Marjorie Proops
3. Teresa Gorman
4. The Duchess of Kent
5. Joan Collins
6. Fay Weldon
7. Angela Thorne
8. Germaine Greer
9. Lizzie Webb
10. Jill Gascoine
11. Stephanie Beacham
12. Dr Miriam Stoppard
13. Isla Blair
14. Judy Finnigan

2 CELEBRITIES WHO WERE NATURISTS

1. Benjamin Franklin
2. Peter Adamson

1 CELEBRITY WHO WAS 26 BEFORE HE FOUND OUT ABOUT MENSTRUATION

1. Sir Alfred Hitchcock. He only found out beause an actress refused to go into the water because ". . ... it was the wrong time of the month".

13 CELEBRITIES WHO LOST THEIR VIRGINITY WITH ANOTHER CELEBRITY

1. Mary Astor with John Barrymore Senior
2. Debbie Reynolds with Eddie Fisher
3. Ava Gardner with Mickey Rooney
4. Nastassja Kinski with Roman Polanski
5. Brigitte Bardot with Roger Vadim
6. Malcolm Maclaren with Vivienne Westwood
7. Julie Burchill with Tony Parsons
8. Cecil Beaton with Adele Astaire
9. Elliot Gould with Barbra Streisand
10. Brooke Shields with Dean Cain
11. Priscilla Beaulieu with Elvis Presley
12. Terry Moore with Howard Hughes
13. Gloria Swanson with Wallace Beery

12 RELATIONSHIPS BETWEEN TWO CELEBRITIES OF WHICH YOU MIGHT NOT HAVE BEEN AWARE

1. Jodie Foster & Scott Baio
2. Jean Seberg & Clint Eastwood (whilst making *Paint Your Wagon*)
3. Keith Allen & Julia Sawalha
4. Rowan Atkinson & Leslie Ash
5. Aristotle Onassis & Eva Peron
6. Ivan Lendl & Pamella Bordes
7. Jack Johnson & Mata Hari
8. Milton Berle & Aimee Semple McPherson
9. Kris Kristofferson & Janis Joplin
10. Robert Kennedy & Jayne Mansfield
11. Amanda Donohoe & Adam Ant
12. Wayne Sleep & Sarah Brightman

Chapter 3

Romantic Liaisons I

6 CELEBRITIES ROMANTICALLY LINKED WITH PAMELA ANDERSON LEE

1. Scott Baio
2. Dean Cain
3. David Charvet
4. Jon Peters
5. Sylvester Stallone
6. Tommy Lee (married)

3 CELEBRITIES ROMANTICALLY LINKED WITH FRANCESCA ANNIS

1. Ralph Fiennes
2. Ian Ogilvy
3. Trevor Eve

9 CELEBRITIES ROMANTICALLY LINKED WITH URSULA ANDRESS

1. James Dean
2. Ryan O'Neal
3. Harry Hamlin
4. Jean-Paul Belmondo
5. Marlon Brando
6. Dennis Hopper
7. Marcello Mastroianni
8. John De Lorean
9. John Derek (married)

3 CELEBRITIES ROMANTICALLY LINKED WITH LESLIE ASH

1. Rowan Atkinson
2. Dave Stewart
3. Lee Chapman (married)

8 CELEBRITIES ROMANTICALLY LINKED WITH LAUREN BACALL

1. Adlai Stevenson
2. Humphrey Bogart (married)
3. Jason Robards (married)
4. Harry Guardino
5. Frank Sinatra
6. Kirk Douglas
7. James Garner
8. Burgess Meredith

5 CELEBRITIES ROMANTICALLY LINKED WITH MARY ASTOR

1. John Barrymore
2. George S. Kaufman
3. John Huston
4. Clark Gable
5. Ronald Colman

10 CELEBRITIES ROMANTICALLY LINKED WITH JOSEPHINE BAKER

1. Max Reinhardt
2. Pablo Picasso
3. Luigi Pirandello
4. Georges Simenon
5. Duke Ellington
6. Ernest Hemingway
7. Maurice Chevalier
8. Colette
9. George Balanchine
10. Le Corbusier

9 CELEBRITIES ROMANTICALLY LINKED WITH LUCILLE BALL

1. Broderick Crawford
2. Henry Fonda
3. George Sanders
4. Peter Lawford
5. Robert Mitchum
6. George Raft
7. Franchot Tone
8. Desi Arnaz (married)
9. Orson Welles

8 CELEBRITIES ROMANTICALLY LINKED WITH BRIGITTE BARDOT

1. Sacha Distel
2. Serge Gainsbourg
3. Louis Malle
4. Gunther Sachs (married)
5. Michael Sarne
6. Jean-Louis Trintignant
7. Roger Vadim (married)
8. Raf Vallone

7 CELEBRITIES ROMANTICALLY LINKED WITH KIM BASINGER

1. Alec Baldwin (married)
2. Jeff Bridges
3. Richard Gere
4. Michael Keaton
5. Prince
6. Robert Redford
7. Mickey Rourke

3 CELEBRITIES ROMANTICALLY LINKED WITH STEPHANIE BEACHAM

1. Eric Clapton
2. Imran Khan
3. Peter McEnery (married)

6 CELEBRITIES ROMANTICALLY LINKED WITH CANDICE BERGEN

1. Lou Adler
2. Louis Malle (married)
3. Warren Beatty
4. Terence Stamp
5. Jerry Brown
6. Jack Nicholson

5 CELEBRITIES ROMANTICALLY LINKED WITH ANN-MARGRET

1. Eddie Fisher
2. Elvis Presley
3. Lou Adler
4. Steve McQueen
5. Johnny Carson

10 CELEBRITIES ROMANTICALLY LINKED WITH TALLULAH BANKHEAD

1. Gary Cooper
2. Douglas Fairbanks Junior
3. Burgess Meredith
4. Johnny Weissmuller
5. John Barrymore Senior
6. Billie Holiday
7. Hattie McDaniel
8. Leonard Bernstein
9. Beatrice Lillie
10. Dame Sybil Thorndyke

9 CELEBRITIES ROMANTICALLY LINKED WITH INGRID BERGMAN

1. Robert Capa
2. Gary Cooper
3. Roberto Rossellini (married)
4. Larry Adler
5. Leslie Howard
6. Bing Crosby
7. Yul Brynner
8. Joseph Cotten
9. Anthony Quinn

4 CELEBRITIES ROMANTICALLY LINKED WITH ANDREA BOARDMAN

1. Darren Day
2. Chris Evans
3. Robbie Fowler
4. Gary Davies

4 CELEBRITIES ROMANTICALLY LINKED WITH JACQUELINE BISSET

1. Ryan O'Neal
2. Alexander Godunov
3. Dean Martin
4. Terence Stamp

8 CELEBRITIES ROMANTICALLY LINKED WITH CLARA BOW

1. Eddie Cantor
2. Gary Cooper
3. Victor Fleming
4. John Gilbert
5. Fredric March
6. Bela Lugosi
7. Tom Mix
8. John Wayne

9 CELEBRITIES ROMANTICALLY LINKED WITH NAOMI CAMPBELL

1. Robert De Niro
2. Prince
3. Eddie Murphy
4. Eric Clapton
5. Sylvester Stallone
6. Mike Tyson
7. Sean Penn
8. Adam Clayton
9. Joaquin Cortés

8 CELEBRITIES ROMANTICALLY LINKED WITH CHER

1. Sonny Bono (married)
2. Greg Allman (married)
3. Val Kilmer
4. Warren Beatty
5. John Heard
6. Gene Simmons
7. Richie Sambora
8. David Geffen

9 CELEBRITIES ROMANTICALLY LINKED WITH JOAN COLLINS

1. Warren Beatty
2. Anthony Newley (married)
3. Ryan O'Neal
4. Terence Stamp
5. Harry Belafonte
6. Marlon Brando
7. Robert Evans
8. Nicky Hilton
9. Robert Wagner

2 CELEBRITIES ROMANTICALLY LINKED WITH COURTNEY COX

1. Michael Keaton
2. David Duchovny

4 CELEBRITIES ROMANTICALLY LINKED WITH CINDY CRAWFORD

1. Richard Gere (married)
2. Val Kilmer
3. Don Johnson
4. Alec Baldwin

23 CELEBRITIES ROMANTICALLY LINKED WITH JOAN CRAWFORD

1. Jackie Cooper
2. Douglas Fairbanks Junior (married)
3. Clark Gable
4. Franchot Tone (married)
5. John F. Kennedy
6. Yul Brynner
7. Kirk Douglas
8. Henry Fonda
9. Glenn Ford
10. John Wayne
11. Cary Grant
12. Joseph Mankiewicz
13. Tyrone Power
14. Robert Preston
15. Barbara Stanwyck
16. John Garfield
17. Jackie Gleason
18. Spencer Tracy
19. Johnny Weissmuller
20. Gary Cooper
21. Jeff Chandler
22. Van Heflin
23. Martha Raye

3 CELEBRITIES ROMANTICALLY LINKED WITH TESSA DAHL

1. David Hemmings
2. Dai Llewellyn
3. Peter Sellers

4 CELEBRITIES ROMANTICALLY LINKED WITH BETTE DAVIS

1. Henry Fonda
2. Howard Hughes
3. Johnny Mercer
4. Franchot Tone

3 CELEBRITIES ROMANTICALLY LINKED WITH JULIA CARLING

1. Eric Clapton

2. Jeff Beck

3. Will Carling (married)

5 CELEBRITIES ROMANTICALLY LINKED WITH JUDY CARNE

1. Burt Reynolds (married)

2. Steve McQueen

3. Vidal Sassoon

4. Warren Beatty

5. Anthony Newley

8 CELEBRITIES ROMANTICALLY LINKED WITH CATHERINE DENEUVE

1. David Bailey (married)

2. Roger Vadim

3. Dean Martin

4. Marcello Mastroianni

5. Omar Sharif

6. Burt Reynolds

7. Roman Polanski

8. Johnny Hallyday

3 CELEBRITIES ROMANTICALLY LINKED WITH LAURA DERN

1. Nicolas Cage
2. Jeff Goldblum
3. Kyle MacLachlan

6 CELEBRITIES ROMANTICALLY LINKED WITH ANGIE DICKINSON

1. Burt Bacharach (married)
2. Frank Sinatra
3. David Janssen
4. John F. Kennedy
5. Johnny Carson
6. Larry King

30 CELEBRITIES ROMANTICALLY LINKED WITH MARLENE DIETRICH

1. Brian Aherne
2. Burt Bacharach
3. Yul Brynner
4. Gary Cooper
5. Mercedes D'Acosta
6. Douglas Fairbanks Jr
7. Eddie Fisher
8. Jean Gabin
9. Erich Maria Remarque
10. James Stewart
11. Mike Todd
12. John Wayne
13. Michael Wilding
14. John F. Kennedy
15. Adlai Stevenson
16. Ronald Colman
17. Robert Donat
18. Edith Piaf
19. Orson Welles
20. Barbara Stanwyck
21. George Raft
22. Maurice Chevalier
23. Fritz Lang
24. John Gilbert
25. Ed Murrow
26. Harry Cohn
27. Sam Spiegel
28. Charles De Gaulle
29. General George Patton
30. Kirk Douglas

12 CELEBRITIES ROMANTICALLY LINKED WITH BRITT EKLAND

1. Warren Beatty
2. George Hamilton
3. Lord Patrick Lichfield
4. Ryan O'Neal
5. Peter Sellers (married)
6. Slim Jim McDonnell (married)
7. Rod Stewart
8. Dodi Fayed
9. Les McKeown
10. Lou Adler
11. Ron Ely
12. Lee Majors

3 CELEBRITIES ROMANTICALLY LINKED WITH SALLY FABER

1. James Hewitt
2. Earl Spencer
3. Kim Bailey

3 CELEBRITIES ROMANTICALLY LINKED WITH FARRAH FAWCETT

1. Ryan O'Neal
2. Lee Majors (married)
3. Sylvester Stallone

9 CELEBRITIES ROMANTICALLY LINKED WITH MIA FARROW

1. Woody Allen
2. Frank Sinatra (married)
3. Andre Previn (married)
4. Sir Tom Stoppard
5. Roman Polanski
6. Leslie Bricusse
7. Eddie Fisher
8. Peter Sellers
9. John Phillips

4 CELEBRITIES ROMANTICALLY LINKED WITH ISABEL FONSECA

1. Martin Amis
2. John Malkovich
3. Clive James
4. Salman Rushdie

10 CELEBRITIES ROMANTICALLY LINKED WITH AVA GARDNER

1. Howard Hughes
2. Mickey Rooney (married)
3. Artie Shaw (married)
4. Frank Sinatra (married)
5. George C. Scott
6. Clark Gable
7. Farley Granger
8. Peter Lawford
9. David Niven
10. Mel Tormé

14 CELEBRITIES ROMANTICALLY LINKED WITH JUDY GARLAND

1. Vincente Minnelli (married)
2. Glenn Ford
3. Jackie Cooper
4. Eddie Fisher
5. Joe Mankiewicz
6. Tyrone Power
7. Frank Sinatra
8. Orson Welles
9. Yul Brynner
10. Prince Aly Khan
11. Maria Lanza
12. Peter Lawford
13. Artie Shaw
14. Ethel Merman

6 CELEBRITIES ROMANTICALLY LINKED WITH ZSA ZSA GABOR

1. George Sanders (married)
2. Richard Burton
3. John F. Kennedy
4. Frank Sinatra
5. Franchot Tone
6. Conrad Hilton (married)

6 CELEBRITIES ROMANTICALLY LINKED WITH SUSAN GEORGE

1. Prince Charles
2. Simon MacCorkindale (married)
3. Jack Jones
4. Andy Gibb
5. George Best
6. Frazer Hines

11 CELEBRITIES ROMANTICALLY LINKED WITH SABRINA GUINNESS

1. Mick Jagger
2. David Bowie
3. Bryan Ferry
4. Jack Nicholson
5. Michael Douglas
6. Jonathan Aitken
7. Jamie Blandford
8. Dai Llewellyn
9. Rod Stewart
10. Bob Geldof
11. Prince Charles

7 CELEBRITIES ROMANTICALLY LINKED WITH RITA HAYWORTH

1. Kirk Douglas
2. Orson Welles (married)
3. Prince Aly Khan (married)
4. Howard Hughes
5. Victor Mature
6. David Niven
7. Robert Mitchum

3 CELEBRITIES ROMANTICALLY LINKED WITH MARIE HELVIN

1. David Bailey (married)
2. Peter Gabriel
3. Eric Clapton

8 CELEBRITIES ROMANTICALLY LINKED WITH JANIS JOPLIN

1. Dick Cavett
2. Kris Kristofferson
3. Country Joe MacDonald
4. Joe Namath
5. Michael J. Pollard
6. Eric Clapton
7. Jimi Hendrix
8. Jim Morrison

10 CELEBRITIES ROMANTICALLY LINKED WITH GRACE KELLY

1. Prince Rainier (married)
2. Oleg Cassini
3. Spencer Tracy
4. Bing Crosby
5. Clark Gable
6. William Holden
7. Prince Aly Khan
8. Cary Grant
9. David Niven
10. Ray Milland

2 CELEBRITIES ROMANTICALLY LINKED WITH ELLE MACPHERSON

1. Sean Penn
2. Kevin Costner

5 CELEBRITIES ROMANTICALLY LINKED WITH PATSY KENSIT

1. Liam Gallagher (married)
2. Jim Kerr (married)
3. Michael Hutchence
4. Eric Clapton
5. Ryan Giggs

10 CELEBRITIES ROMANTICALLY LINKED WITH MADONNA

1. Warren Beatty
2. Sean Penn (married)
3. Sylvester Stallone
4. Prince
5. Mickey Rourke
6. Sandra Bernhard
7. Dennis Rodman
8. Jack Nicholson
9. Daniel Day-Lewis
10. Julian Sands

6 CELEBRITIES ROMANTICALLY LINKED WITH JANE FONDA

1. Roger Vadim (married)
2. Ted Turner (married)
3. Alain Delon
4. Donald Sutherland
5. Warren Beatty
6. James Franciscus

8 CELEBRITIES ROMANTICALLY LINKED WITH GRETA GARBO

1. John Gilbert
2. Dolores Del Rio
3. Cecil Beaton
4. Joseph Kennedy
5. Ramon Navarro
6. Beatrice Lillie
7. Erich Maria Remarque
8. Leopold Stokowski

6 CELEBRITIES ROMANTICALLY LINKED WITH AUDREY HEPBURN

1. Mel Ferrer (married)
2. John F. Kennedy
3. Albert Finney
4. Ben Gazzara
5. William Holden
6. Lord Hanson

5 CELEBRITIES ROMANTICALLY LINKED WITH NASTASSJA KINSKI

1. Roman Polanski
2. Gerard Depardieu
3. Quincy Jones
4. Marcello Mastroianni
5. Dudley Moore

6 CELEBRITIES ROMANTICALLY LINKED WITH LISE MAYER

1. Angus Deayton
2. Rik Mayall
3. Jack Docherty
4. Harry Enfield
5. Rowan Atkinson
6. Hugh Laurie

6 CELEBRITIES ROMANTICALLY LINKED WITH JACKIE ONASSIS

1. John F. Kennedy (married)
2. Aristotle Onassis (married)
3. Robert F. Kennedy
4. Marlon Brando
5. Warren Beatty
6. William Holden

5 CELEBRITIES ROMANTICALLY LINKED WITH MICHELLE PFEIFFER

1. Michael Keaton
2. John Malkovich
3. Kiefer Sutherland
4. Eric Clapton
5. Kevin Costner

21 CELEBRITIES ROMANTICALLY LINKED WITH MARILYN MONROE

1. Marlon Brando
2. John F. Kennedy
3. Robert Kennedy
4. Arthur Miller (married)
5. Joe DiMaggio (married)
6. Harry Cohn
7. Yves Montand
8. Frank Sinatra
9. Milton Berle
10. Yul Brynner
11. Sammy Davis Junior
12. Bugsy Siegel
13. Howard Hughes
14. John Huston
15. Dean Martin
16. Robert Mitchum
17. Mickey Rooney
18. George Sanders
19. Orson Welles
20. Mel Tormé
21. Oleg Cassini

7 CELEBRITIES ROMANTICALLY LINKED WITH JULIA ROBERTS

1. Lyle Lovett (married)
2. Ethan Hawke
3. Daniel Day-Lewis
4. Jason Patric
5. Liam Neeson
6. Kiefer Sutherland
7. Michael Bolton

4 CELEBRITIES ROMANTICALLY LINKED WITH ISABELLA ROSSELLINI

1. Gary Oldman (married)
2. David Lynch
3. Martin Scorsese (married)
4. Mikhail Baryshnikov

8 CELEBRITIES ROMANTICALLY LINKED WITH BARBARA STANWYCK

1. Joan Crawford
2. Marlene Dietrich
3. Glenn Ford
4. Al Jolson
5. William Holden
6. Frank Capra
7. Robert Taylor (married)
8. Gary Cooper

5 CELEBRITIES ROMANTICALLY LINKED WITH WINONA RYDER

1. Daniel Day-Lewis
2. Johnny Depp
3. David Duchovny
4. Christian Slater
5. Dodi Fayed

10 CELEBRITIES ROMANTICALLY LINKED WITH ELIZABETH TAYLOR

1. Richard Burton (married, twice)
2. Eddie Fisher (married)
3. Stanley Donen
4. Rod Steiger
5. Mike Todd (married)
6. Michael Wilding (married)
7. George Hamilton
8. Vic Damone
9. Frank Sinatra
10. Nicky Hilton (married)

6 CELEBRITIES ROMANTICALLY LINKED WITH UMA THURMAN

1. Mick Jagger
2. Gary Oldman (married)
3. Robert De Niro
4. Nicolas Cage
5. Judd Nelson
6. Ethan Hawke

4 CELEBRITIES ROMANTICALLY LINKED WITH DIANA, PRINCESS OF WALES

1. Prince Charles (married)
2. James Hewitt
3. Dodi Fayed
4. Will Carling

17 CELEBRITIES ROMANTICALLY LINKED WITH LANA TURNER

1. Lex Barker (married)
2. Artie Shaw (married)
3. Richard Burton
4. Frank Sinatra
5. Robert Wagner
6. Mickey Rooney
7. Tommy Dorsey
8. Peter Lawford
9. Tyrone Power
10. Mel Tormé
11. Clark Gable
12. Dean Martin
13. John Garfield
14. John F. Kennedy
15. Howard Hughes
16. Leonard Bernstein
17. Victor Mature

4 CELEBRITIES ROMANTICALLY LINKED WITH MARTINE McCUTCHEON

1. Mick Hucknall
2. John Pickard
3. Paul Nicholls
4. Will Mellor

14 CELEBRITIES ROMANTICALLY LINKED WITH BARBRA STREISAND

1. Richard Gere
2. Andre Agassi
3. James Brolin (married)
4. Elliott Gould (married)
5. Don Johnson
6. Warren Beatty
7. Ryan O'Neal
8. Kris Kristofferson
9. Pierre Trudeau
10. Omar Sharif
11. Anthony Newley
12. Jon Peters (married)
13. George Lucas
14. Liam Neeson

4 CELEBRITIES ROMANTICALLY LINKED WITH LADY JANE WELLESLEY

1. Prince Charles
2. Lord Patrick Lichfield
3. Melvyn Bragg
4. Andrew Parker-Bowles

6 CELEBRITIES ROMANTICALLY LINKED WITH CAROL WHITE

1. Adam Faith
2. John Barry
3. Oliver Reed
4. Warren Beatty
5. Peter Sellers
6. Richard O'Sullivan

3 CELEBRITIES ROMANTICALLY LINKED WITH KIM WILDE

1. Chris Evans
2. Mick Hucknall
3. Hal Fowler (married)

6 CELEBRITIES ROMANTICALLY LINKED WITH BARBARA WINDSOR

1. Ronnie Knight (married)
2. Maurice Gibb
3. John Reid
4. Gary Crosby
5. Sid James
6. Charlie Kray

11 CELEBRITIES ROMANTICALLY LINKED WITH SHELLEY WINTERS

1. Burt Lancaster
2. Marlon Brando
3. Errol Flynn
4. Farley Granger
5. William Holden
6. Sean Connery
7. Albert Finney
8. Clark Gable
9. Howard Hughes
10. Vittorio Gassman (married)
11. Anthony Franciosa (married)

6 CELEBRITIES ROMANTICALLY LINKED WITH NATALIE WOOD

1. Robert Wagner (married, twice)
2. Steve McQueen
3. Robert Vaughn
4. James Dean
5. Warren Beatty
6. Elvis Presley

Chapter 4

Romantic Liaisons II

34 CELEBRITIES ROMANTICALLY LINKED WITH WARREN BEATTY

1. Leslie Caron
2. Julie Christie
3. Joan Collins
4. Britt Ekland
5. Anjelica Huston
6. Diane Keaton
7. Joni Mitchell
8. Michelle Phillips
9. Susan Strasberg
10. Barbra Streisand
11. Natalie Wood
12. Annette Bening (married)
13. Madonna
14. Goldie Hawn
15. Jackie Onassis
16. Judy Carne
17. Cher
18. Isabelle Adjani
19. Brigitte Bardot
20. Candice Bergen
21. Melanie Griffith
22. Jane Fonda
23. Diana Ross
24. Carly Simon
25. Liv Ullmann
26. Kate Jackson
27. Carol White
28. Bianca Jagger
29. Vivien Leigh
30. Christina Onassis
31. Vanessa Redgrave
32. Jean Seberg
33. Barbara Harris
34. Lee Radziwill

6 CELEBRITIES ROMANTICALLY LINKED WITH JERRY BROWN

1. Linda Ronstadt
2. Liv Ullmann
3. Arianna Stassinopoulos
4. Natalie Wood
5. Candice Bergen
6. Stevie Nicks

10 CELEBRITIES ROMANTICALLY LINKED WITH YUL BRYNNER

1. Tallulah Bankhead
2. Ingrid Bergman
3. Joan Crawford
4. Marlene Dietrich
5. Judy Garland
6. Gina Lollobrigida
7. Marilyn Monroe
8. Nancy Reagan
9. Anne Baxter
10. Yvonne De Carlo

8 CELEBRITIES ROMANTICALLY LINKED WITH RICHARD BURTON

1. Claire Bloom
2. Genevieve Bujold
3. Sophia Loren
4. Jean Simmons
5. Susan Strasberg
6. Elizabeth Taylor (married, twice)
7. Zsa Zsa Gabor
8. Lana Turner

3 CELEBRITIES ROMANTICALLY LINKED WITH NICOLAS CAGE

1. Patricia Arquette (married)
2. Laura Dern
3. Uma Thurman

8 CELEBRITIES ROMANTICALLY LINKED WITH CHARLIE CHAPLIN

1. Marion Davies
2. Paulette Goddard (married)
3. Oona O'Neill (married)
4. Hedy Lamarr
5. Carole Landis
6. Pola Negri
7. Lupe Velez
8. Louise Brooks

12 CELEBRITIES ROMANTICALLY LINKED WITH GARY COOPER

1. Ingrid Bergman
2. Tallulah Bankhead
3. Clara Bow
4. Marlene Dietrich
5. Carole Lombard
6. Patricia Neal
7. Mae West
8. Joan Crawford
9. Claudette Colbert
10. Paulette Goddard
11. Merle Oberon
12. Barbara Stanwyck

3 CELEBRITIES ROMANTICALLY LINKED WITH DARREN DAY

1. Andrea Boardman
2. Tracy Shaw
3. Anna Friel

7 CELEBRITIES ROMANTICALLY LINKED WITH BING CROSBY

1. Ingrid Bergman
2. Joan Blondell
3. Frances Farmer
4. Betty Hutton
5. Grace Kelly
6. Dorothy Lamour
7. Joan Bennett

3 CELEBRITIES ROMANTICALLY LINKED WITH ANGUS DEAYTON

1. Helen Atkinson-Wood
2. Stephanie de Sykes
3. Lise Mayer

8 CELEBRITIES ROMANTICALLY LINKED WITH DANIEL DAY-LEWIS

1. Julia Roberts
2. Juliette Binoche
3. Winona Ryder
4. Isabelle Adjani
5. Greta Scaachi
6. Madonna
7. Sinead O'Connor
8. Rebecca Miller

6 CELEBRITIES ROMANTICALLY LINKED WITH CHRIS EVANS

1. Kim Wilde
2. Andrea Boardman
3. Rachel Tatton-Brown
4. Suzi Aplin
5. Carol McGiffin (married)
6. Anthea Turner

12 CELEBRITIES ROMANTICALLY LINKED WITH DODI FAYED

1. Diana, Princess of Wales
2. Koo Stark
3. Susannah Constantine
4. Tracey Ward
5. Joanne Whalley-Kilmer
6. Brooke Shields
7. Valerie Perrine
8. Britt Ekland
9. Julia Roberts
10. Tania Bryer
11. Winona Ryder
12. Tina Sinatra

11 CELEBRITIES ROMANTICALLY LINKED WITH EDDIE FISHER

1. Ann-Margret
2. Marlene Dietrich
3. Judy Garland
4. Merle Oberon
5. Stephanie Powers
6. Juliet Prowse
7. Debbie Reynolds (married)
8. Maria Schell
9. Elizabeth Taylor (married)
10. Connie Stevens (married)
11. Michelle Phillips

7 CELEBRITIES ROMANTICALLY LINKED WITH KIRK DOUGLAS

1. Marlene Dietrich
2. Joan Crawford
3. Evelyn Keyes
4. Rita Hayworth
5. Patricia Neal
6. Gene Tierney
7. Lana Turner

14 CELEBRITIES ROMANTICALLY LINKED WITH ERIC CLAPTON

1. Susannah Doyle
2. Julia Carling
3. Paula Hamilton
4. Marie Helvin
5. Patsy Kensit
6. Catrina Skepper
7. Stephanie Beacham
8. Michelle Phillips
9. Janis Joplin
10. Carla Bruni
11. Naomi Campbell
12. Sheryl Crow
13. Michelle Pfeiffer
14. Patti Boyd Harrison (married)

3 CELEBRITIES ROMANTICALLY LINKED WITH JOHNNY DEPP

1. Winona Ryder
2. Sherilyn Fenn
3. Kate Moss

4 CELEBRITIES ROMANTICALLY LINKED WITH ROBERT DE NIRO

1. Naomi Campbell
2. Whitney Houston
3. Ashley Judd
4. Uma Thurman

5 CELEBRITIES ROMANTICALLY LINKED WITH DOUGLAS FAIRBANKS JR

1. Joan Crawford (married)
2. Tallulah Bankhead
3. Marlene Dietrich
4. Gertrude Lawrence
5. Loretta Young

11 CELEBRITIES ROMANTICALLY LINKED WITH ERROL FLYNN

1. Truman Capote
2. Gloria Vanderbilt
3. Eva Peron
4. Tyrone Power
5. Shelley Winters
6. Joan Bennett
7. Virginia Hill
8. Barbara Hutton
9. Hedy Lamarr
10. Carole Landis
11. Ann Sheridan

16 CELEBRITIES ROMANTICALLY LINKED WITH CLARK GABLE

1. Joan Crawford
2. Carole Lombard (married)
3. Marion Davies
4. Ava Gardner
5. Paulette Goddard
6. Jean Harlow
7. Hedy Lamarr
8. Grace Kelly
9. Merle Oberon
10. Nancy Reagan
11. Norma Shearer
12. Lana Turner
13. Shelley Winters
14. Loretta Young
15. Yvonne De Carlo
16. Louella Parsons

9 CELEBRITIES ROMANTICALLY LINKED WITH RICHARD GERE

1. Cindy Crawford (married)
2. Laura Bailey
3. Uma Thurman
4. Barbra Streisand
5. Kim Basinger
6. Diana Ross
7. Tuesday Weld
8. Barbara Carrera
9. Priscilla Presley

2 CELEBRITIES ROMANTICALLY LINKED WITH RYAN GIGGS

1. Davinia Murphy
2. Dani Behr

8 CELEBRITIES ROMANTICALLY LINKED WITH GEORGE HAMILTON

1. Britt Ekland
2. Alana Hamilton (married)
3. Elizabeth Taylor
4. Imelda Marcos
5. Vanessa Redgrave
6. Sylvia Kristel
7. Françoise Pascal
8. Jeanne Moreau

9 CELEBRITIES ROMANTICALLY LINKED WITH WILLIAM HOLDEN

1. Audrey Hepburn
2. Grace Kelly
3. Stephanie Powers
4. Capucine (notwithstanding her lesbian preferences)
5. Susan Hayward
6. Dorothy Lamour
7. Barbara Stanwyck
8. Shelley Winters
9. Jackie Onassis (before she married JFK)

5 CELEBRITIES ROMANTICALLY LINKED WITH MICK HUCKNALL

1. Kim Wilde
2. Helena Christensen
3. Martine McCutcheon
4. Kathy Lloyd
5. Catherine Zeta Jones

27 CELEBRITIES ROMANTICALLY LINKED WITH HOWARD HUGHES

1. Linda Darnell
2. Terry Moore (married)
3. Jean Peters (married)
4. Katharine Hepburn
5. Ginger Rogers
6. Ida Lupino
7. Lana Turner
8. Hedy Lamarr
9. Olivia De Havilland
10. Jean Harlow
11. Rita Hayworth
12. Bette Davis
13. Yvonne De Carlo
14. Susan Hayward
15. Barbara Hutton
16. Carole Lombard
17. Marilyn Monroe
18. Luise Rainer
19. Norma Shearer
20. Constance Talmadge
21. Gene Tierney
22. Gloria Vanderbilt
23. Shelley Winters
24. Fay Wray
25. Cary Grant
26. Joan Fontaine
27. Tyrone Power

Note: Howard Hughes married Jean Peters and Terry Moore. Jean Peters's previous husband was Stuart Cramer III. One of Terry Moore's later husbands was . . . Stuart Cramer III.

15 CELEBRITIES ROMANTICALLY LINKED WITH MICK JAGGER

1. Bianca Jagger (married)
2. Jerry Hall (married)
3. Marsha Hunt
4. Carla Bruni
5. Brigitte Bardot
6. Marianne Faithfull
7. Sabrina Guinness
8. Patti La Belle
9. Linda Ronstadt
10. Carly Simon
11. Uma Thurman
12. Margaret Trudeau
13. Madonna
14. Patti D'Arbanville
15. Chrissie Shrimpton

4 CELEBRITIES ROMANTICALLY LINKED WITH ELLIOT GOULD

1. Barbra Streisand (married)

2. Bianca Jagger

3. Valerie Perrine

4. Jennifer O'Neill

7 CELEBRITIES ROMANTICALLY LINKED WITH IMRAN KHAN

1. Susannah Constantine

2. Jemima Goldsmith (married)

3. Jerry Hall

4. Emma Sergeant

5. Stephanie Beacham

6. Goldie Hawn

7. Marie Helvin

10 CELEBRITIES ROMANTICALLY LINKED WITH CARY GRANT

1. Dyan Cannon (married)

2. Ginger Rogers

3. Sophia Loren

4. Kim Novak

5. Grace Kelly

6. Susan Strasberg

7. Randolph Scott

8. Mae West

9. Fay Wray

10. Howard Hughes

5 CELEBRITIES ROMANTICALLY LINKED WITH MARCELLO MASTROIANNI

1. Faye Dunaway
2. Catherine Deneuve
3. Nastassja Kinski
4. Jeanne Moreau
5. Susan Strasberg

2 CELEBRITIES ROMANTICALLY LINKED WITH ROB LOWE

1. Princess Stephanie of Monaco
2. Chynna Phillips

5 CELEBRITIES ROMANTICALLY LINKED WITH DON JOHNSON

1. Melanie Griffith (married)
2. Barbra Streisand
3. Patti D'Arbanville
4. Oprah Winfrey
5. Cindy Crawford

14 CELEBRITIES ROMANTICALLY LINKED WITH JOHN F. KENNEDY

1. June Allyson
2. Joan Crawford
3. Angie Dickinson
4. Marlene Dietrich
5. Gene Tierney
6. Norma Shearer
7. Zsa Zsa Gabor
8. Marilyn Monroe
9. Jayne Mansfield
10. Sonja Henie
11. Audrey Hepburn
12. Lee Remick
13. Susan Hayward
14. Lana Turner

4 CELEBRITIES ROMANTICALLY LINKED WITH VAL KILMER

1. Elisabeth Shue
2. Joanne Whalley-Kilmer (married)
3. Cindy Crawford
4. Cher

5 CELEBRITIES ROMANTICALLY LINKED WITH STEVE McQUEEN

1. Ali MacGraw
2. Judy Carne
3. Natalie Wood
4. Faye Dunaway
5. Ann-Margret

8 CELEBRITIES ROMANTICALLY LINKED WITH ROBERT MITCHUM

1. Lucille Ball
2. Carroll Baker
3. Rita Hayworth
4. Gloria Grahame
5. Ava Gardner
6. Shirley Maclaine
7. Marilyn Monroe
8. Jean Simmons

5 CELEBRITIES ROMANTICALLY LINKED WITH LIAM NEESON

1. Julia Roberts
2. Helen Mirren
3. Brooke Shields
4. Barbra Streisand
5. Natasha Richardson (married)

2 CELEBRITIES ROMANTICALLY LINKED WITH FRANCO NERO

1. Vanessa Redgrave
2. Carroll Baker

3 CELEBRITIES ROMANTICALLY LINKED WITH NEIL PEARSON

1. Susannah Doyle
2. Frances Barber
3. Siobhan Redmond

19 CELEBRITIES ROMANTICALLY LINKED WITH DAVID NIVEN

1. Paulette Goddard
2. Vivien Leigh
3. Ava Gardner
4. Doris Duke
5. Rita Hayworth
6. Barbara Hutton
7. Grace Kelly
8. Evelyn Keyes
9. Deborah Kerr
10. Hedy Lamarr
11. Carole Lombard
12. Ida Lupino
13. Merle Oberon
14. Ginger Rogers
15. Norma Shearer
16. Ann Sheridan
17. Ann Todd
18. Mae West
19. Loretta Young

7 CELEBRITIES ROMANTICALLY LINKED WITH SEAN PENN

1. Madonna (married)
2. Sandra Bernhard
3. Elle Macpherson
4. Naomi Campbell
5. Mary Stuart Masterson
6. Elizabeth McGovern
7. Robin Wright Penn (married)

9 CELEBRITIES ROMANTICALLY LINKED WITH TYRONE POWER

1. Linda Christian (married)
2. Judy Garland
3. Sonja Henie
4. Mai Zetterling
5. Anita Ekberg
6. Joan Crawford
7. Errol Flynn
8. Howard Hughes
9. Lana Turner

8 CELEBRITIES ROMANTICALLY LINKED WITH BURT REYNOLDS

1. Loni Anderson (married)
2. Dinah Shore
3. Catherine Deneuve
4. Sally Field
5. Candice Bergen
6. Cybill Shepherd
7. Judy Carne (married)
8. Tammy Wynette

7 CELEBRITIES ROMANTICALLY LINKED WITH ELVIS PRESLEY

1. Priscilla Presley (married)
2. Tuesday Weld
3. Juliet Prowse
4. Ann-Margret
5. Jayne Mansfield
6. Cybill Shepherd
7. Natalie Wood

3 CELEBRITIES ROMANTICALLY LINKED WITH GEORGE SANDERS

1. Zsa Zsa Gabor (married)
2. Magda Gabor (married)
3. Lucille Ball

3 CELEBRITIES ROMANTICALLY LINKED WITH PRINCE

1. Kim Basinger
2. Naomi Campbell
3. Madonna

4 CELEBRITIES ROMANTICALLY LINKED WITH PETER SELLERS

1. Lynne Frederick (married)
2. Britt Ekland (married)
3. Tessa Dahl
4. Carol White

5 CELEBRITIES ROMANTICALLY LINKED WITH BRAD PITT

1. Gwyneth Paltrow
2. Robin Givens
3. Geena Davis
4. Sinitta
5. Nicole Appleton

5 CELEBRITIES ROMANTICALLY LINKED WITH LORD PATRICK LICHFIELD

1. Lady Jane Wellesley
2. Britt Ekland
3. Joanna Lumley
4. Jane Seymour
5. Gayle Hunnicutt

3 CELEBRITIES ROMANTICALLY LINKED WITH ANDREW PARKER-BOWLES

1. Camilla Parker-Bowles (married)
2. Lady Jane Wellesley
3. Princess Anne

10 CELEBRITIES ROMANTICALLY LINKED WITH JACK NICHOLSON

1. Rebecca Broussard
2. Susan Anspach
3. Anjelica Huston
4. Michelle Phillips
5. Margaret Trudeau
6. Candice Bergen
7. Faye Dunaway
8. Madonna
9. Jessica Lange
10. Christina Onassis

5 CELEBRITIES ROMANTICALLY LINKED WITH OMAR SHARIF

1. Anouk Aimee
2. Catherine Deneuve
3. Barbra Streisand
4. Dyan Cannon
5. Julie Christie

5 CELEBRITIES ROMANTICALLY LINKED WITH SYLVESTER STALLONE

1. Madonna
2. Naomi Campbell
3. Brigitte Nielsen (married)
4. Farrah Fawcett
5. Pamela Anderson Lee

6 CELEBRITIES ROMANTICALLY LINKED WITH ROD STEWART

1. Alana Hamilton (married)
2. Rachel Hunter (married)
3. Britt Ekland
4. Kelly Emberg
5. Joanna Lumley
6. Sabrina Guinness

19 CELEBRITIES ROMANTICALLY LINKED WITH FRANK SINATRA

1. Lauren Bacall
2. Angie Dickinson
3. Mia Farrow (married)
4. Ava Gardner (married)
5. Judy Garland
6. Marilyn Monroe
7. Kim Novak
8. Juliet Prowse
9. Jill St John
10. Lana Turner
11. Natalie Wood
12. Anita Ekberg
13. Carol White
14. Nancy Reagan
15. Patty Duke
16. Eva Gabor
17. Zsa Zsa Gabor
18. Shirley Maclaine
19. Tuesday Weld

4 CELEBRITIES ROMANTICALLY LINKED WITH TERENCE STAMP

1. Jean Shrimpton
2. Jacqueline Bisset
3. Candice Bergen
4. Julie Christie

5 CELEBRITIES ROMANTICALLY LINKED WITH PRINCE CHARLES

1. Princess Diana (married)
2. Camilla Parker-Bowles
3. Lady Jane Wellesley
4. Sabrina Guinness
5. Susan George

7 CELEBRITIES ROMANTICALLY LINKED WITH SPENCER TRACY

1. Katharine Hepburn
2. Paulette Goddard
3. Nancy Reagan
4. Joan Crawford
5. Ingrid Bergman
6. Joan Bennett
7. Grace Kelly

4 CELEBRITIES ROMANTICALLY LINKED WITH JOHN WAYNE

1. Joan Crawford
2. Marlene Dietrich
3. Clara Bow
4. Carmen Miranda

4 CELEBRITIES ROMANTICALLY LINKED WITH ROBBIE WILLIAMS

1. Anna Friel
2. Nicole Appleton
3. Natalie Imbruglia
4. Denise Van Outen

8 CELEBRITIES ROMANTICALLY LINKED WITH ORSON WELLES

1. Rita Hayworth (married)
2. Eartha Kitt
3. Marlene Dietrich
4. Judy Garland
5. Marilyn Monroe
6. Lena Horne
7. Gloria Vanderbilt
8. Lucille Ball

Chapter 5

Tying (and Untying) the Knot

━━━━━━━━━━━━━━━

18 CELEBRITIES WHO MARRIED THEIR COUSINS

1. James Boswell

2. Franklin D. Roosevelt

3. Mohammed Sarwar MP

4. Albert Einstein (his second marriage)

5. Lewis Carroll

6. Mary, Queen of Scots

7. Queen Victoria

8. Christopher Robin Milne

9. Satyajit Ray

10. Charles Darwin

11. King Olav V of Norway

12. Sir Edward du Cann

13. Karen Blixen

14. Catherine The Great

15. André Gide

16. H.G. Wells

17. Edgar Allan Poe (she was13)

18. Jerry Lee Lewis (she was13)

21 CELEBRITIES WHO WERE BETROTHED VERY QUICKLY

1. Muhammad Ali. In 1964, he met Sonji Roi and proposed to her on the same day. They married 42 days later.

2. Michael Douglas. In 1977, he met Diandra Luker at Jimmy Carter's Presidential inauguration. They spent two days in his Washington hotel room, he proposed after nine days and they married six weeks later.

3. Peter Noone. In 1967, he married Mireille just six weeks after they met.

4. Sara Crowe. In 1992, she met Toby Dale (son of Jim) on the set of *Carry On Columbus*. He proposed after three weeks and they were married after a month (although a different account has him proposing after eleven weeks and marrying two days later).

5. Fiona Wright. In 1995, she married Mark Chattwell after a ten-day romance. They met at Champneys and he proposed to her after three days. They married seven days later.

6. Marco Pierre White. In 1992, he proposed to Lisa Butcher just three weeks after they met.

7. Daryl Hannah. In 1980, she and Mark Halperin were married in Mexico (although there are doubts whether the marriage was actually registered) just two days after they met.

8. Pamela Anderson. In 1995, she and Tommy Lee decided to marry after a five-day courtship.

9. Leslie Ash. In 1982, she married Jonathan Weston after a two-week courtship.

10. Owen Oyston. In 1962, he married Vicki Burns after going out for just five weeks.

11. Charlie Sheen. In 1995, he married Donna Peele after a six-week courtship.

12. Julia Roberts. In 1993, she married Lyle Lovett after a three-week romance.

13. Kate Jackson. In 1978, she married Andrew Stevens after a six-week courtship.

14. Bienvenida Sokolow. In 1990, she married Sir Antony Buck after a three-week courtship.

15. Drew Barrymore. In 1994, she married Jeremy Thomas after a six-week courtship.

16. Shannen Doherty. In 1993, she married Ashley Hamilton after a two-week romance.

17. John Major. In 1970, he and Norma Wagstaff decided to marry after just three weeks.

18. Lord David Owen. In 1968, he and Debbie Schabert were married after a 26-day courtship.

19. Jim Davidson. He and Alison Holloway were married after a three-week courtship.

20. Judy Geeson. In 1985, she and Kristoffer Tabori were married eight weeks after they met.

21. Raine, Countess Spencer. In 1993, she was proposed to by Count Jean-François de Chambrun, just 33 days after they met.

27 PAIRS OF CELEBRITIES WHO PURPORTEDLY HAD/HAVE OPEN MARRIAGES

1. Aneurin Bevan and Jennie Lee
2. Naomi and Dick Mitchison
3. Harold and Grace Robbins
4. Bertrand Russell and Dora Black
5. Terry and Alison Jones
6. Carl and Emma Jung
7. Jacqueline and John F. Kennedy
8. Leonard and Virginia Woolf
9. Jess and Elaine Yates
10. Paula Yates and Bob Geldof
11. William and Jane Morris
12. Salvador and Gala Dali
13. Harold Nicolson and Vita Sackville-West
14. Denholm and Susan Elliott
15. Lord Louis and Lady Edwina Mountbatten
16. George and Diana Melly (at different times and in different interviews, the great jazz singer and writer has admitted or denied that he and his wife have an open marriage. What is certain is that whatever they do have works extremely well as they've been together for many years)
17. Dmitri and Nina Shostakovich
18. Havelock and Edith Ellis
19. The Marquis and Marchioness of Bath
20. Peter and Margaret Jay
21. Jay and Fran Landesman
22. Marlene Dietrich and Rudolf Sieber
23. Gary and Veronica (Rocky) Cooper
24. Charles Laughton and Elsa Lanchester
25. Sir William and Lady Emma Hamilton
27. Horatio and Fanny Nelson
27. Lyndon and Lady Bird Johnson

28 CELEBRITIES IN UNCONSUMMATED MARRIAGES

1. Mary, Queen of Scots and Prince Francis of France

2. Stanley Spencer and Patricia Preece

3. Sir J.M. Barrie and Mary Ansell

4. Sammy Davis Junior and Loray White

5. Ronnie Kray and Kate Howard

6. George Bernard Shaw and Charlotte Townsend

7. David and Etan Merrick

8. LaToya Jackson and Jack Gordon

9. Eva Bartok and William Wordsworth

10. Burt Lancaster and June Ernst

11. Zsa Zsa Gabor and Burhan Belge

12. Marie Stopes and Reginald Ruggles Gate

13. Prince Arthur (King Henry VIII's older brother) and Catherine of Aragon

14. Jean Harlow and Paul Bern

15. Thomas and Jane Carlyle

16. John Ruskin and Euphemia Gray (He was shocked to discover on their wedding night that she had pubic hair. She eventually left him for the artist John Millais, with whom she had eight children.)

17. Rudolph Valentino and Jean Acker

18. Rudolph Valentino and Natasha Rambova

19. King Henry VIII and Anne of Cleves

20. Peter Tchaikovsky and Antonina Milyukova

21. Catherine and Peter The Great

22. Havelock and Edith Ellis

23. André Gide and Madeleine Rondeaux

24. Mao Tse-Tung and his first wife

25. Paul O'Grady (aka Lily Savage) and Teresa Fernandes

26. Fanny Brice and Frank White

27. Judy Garland and Mark Herron

28. Giuseppe Garibaldi and Giuseppina Raimondi

Note: It took Marie Antoinette and King Louis XVI _seven_ years to consummate their marriage.

9 CELEBRITIES WHO COMMITTED BIGAMY

1. Rudolph Valentino

2. George Gissing

3. John F. Kennedy (it is said that he married a Palm Beach socialite named Durie Malcom in 1939 and was still married to her in 1953 when he married Jacqueline Bouvier)

4. King George III

5. 3rd Baron Moynihan

6. Anaïs Nin

7. Jerry Lee Lewis (at the age of 16!)

8. Judy Garland (unwittingly married Mark Herron in 1964 when she was still married to Sid Luft)

9. Sidney Reilly (aka the Ace of Spies)

3 CELEBRITIES WHO HAD A BIGAMOUS PARENT

1. Dame Cleo Laine (mother)

2. Sir Michael Redgrave (father)

3. Lord Jeffrey Archer (father)

24 CELEBRITIES WHO MARRIED THEIR SECRETARIES

(In the case of dead celebrities, these were not necessarily their last wives; in the case of living celebrities, these are not necessarily their current wives)

1. Peter De Savary
2. Bertrand Russell
3. Jorge Luis Borges
4. Lord Hailsham
5. Christopher Chope
6. Greville Wynne
7. John Biffen
8. T.S. Eliot
9. Burt Lancaster
10. Lord Douglas Hurd
11. Nadim Sawalha
12. Fyodor Dostoevsky
13. Robin Cook
14. Lord Woodrow Wyatt
15. Sir James Goldsmith
16. Thomas Hardy
17. Lord Douglas Jay
18. Sir Peter Hall
19. Jimmy Hill
20. Sir Henry Wood
21. Bryan Gould
22. Hugo Summerson
23. John Stonehouse
24. Lord John Wakeham

5 CELEBRITIES WHO MARRIED THEIR BOSSES

1. Mariah Carey (Tommy Mottola – the boss of her record company)

2. Edwina Currie (Raymond Currie – her boss in an accountancy firm)

3. Debbie McGee (Paul Daniels – her boss in the magic act)

4. Norma Shearer (Irving Thalberg – the boss of MGM)

5. Sally Quinn (Ben Bradlee – her former boss at the *Washington Post*)

21 CELEBRITIES WHO MARRIED THEIR 'CHILDHOOD SWEETHEARTS'

(*= Subsequently divorced or separated)

1. George Segal
2. Robert Smith
3. Glenn Hoddle*
4. Andrew Morton
5. Jon Bon Jovi
6. Tom Jones
7. Bono
8. Les Dennis*
9. Bradley Walsh*
10. Paul Merson
11. Eamonn Holmes*
12. George Carey, Archbishop of Canterbury
13. Nigel Benn*
14. David Blunkett*
15. Michael Parkinson
16. Bruce Rioch
17. Stephen Hendry
18. Harrison Ford*
19. Nick Berry
20. Sally Field*
21. Michael Bolton*

56 PAIRS OF CELEBRITIES WITH A SPOUSE IN COMMON

1. Mia Farrow and Ava Gardner – Frank Sinatra

2. Henry Fonda and William Wyler – Margaret Sullavan

3. Sir Rex Harrison and Richard Harris – Elizabeth Harris

4. Artie Shaw and Lex Barker – Lana Turner

5. Humphrey Bogart and Jason Robards – Lauren Bacall

6. Mimi Rogers and Nicole Kidman – Tom Cruise

7. Ursula Andress and Linda Evans – John Derek

8. Vivien Leigh and Joan Plowright – Sir Laurence Olivier

9. Catherine Deneuve and Marie Helvin – David Bailey

10. Brigitte Bardot and Jane Fonda – Roger Vadim

11. Peter Sellers and Sir David Frost – Lynne Frederick

12. Charlie Chaplin and Burgess Meredith – Paulette Goddard

13. Michael Jayston and Andre Previn – Heather Jayston

14. George Sanders and Ronald Colman – Benita Hume

15. John Huston and Artie Shaw – Evelyn Keyes

16. Laurence Harvey and Michael Wilding – Margaret Leighton

17. Clark Gable and William Powell – Carole Lombard

18. Jeanne Moreau and Lesley–Anne Down – William Friedkin

19. Germaine Greer and Maya Angelou – Paul de Feu

20. Franchot Tone and Douglas Fairbanks Jr. – Joan Crawford

21. Don Johnson and Antonio Banderas – Melanie Griffith

22. W. Somerset Maugham and Henry Wellcome – Syrie Barnardo

23. Elizabeth Taylor and Joan Blondell – Mike Todd

24. Elizabeth Taylor and Debbie Reynolds – Eddie Fisher

25. Rod Steiger and Philip Roth – Claire Bloom

26. Barbara Hutton and Dyan Cannon – Cary Grant

27. Roger Vadim and Ted Turner – Jane Fonda

28. Gloria Swanson and Constance Bennett – Marquis de la Coudraye

29. Myrna Loy and Hedy Lamarr – Gene Markey

30. Judy Carne and Loni Anderson – Burt Reynolds

31. Lana Turner and Arlene Dahl – Lex Barker

32. Nancy Reagan and Jane Wyman – Ronald Reagan

33. Lana Turner and Evelyn Keyes – Artie Shaw

34. Mickey Rooney and Artie Shaw – Ava Gardner

35. Margaret Sullavan and Pamela Harriman – Leland Hayward

36. Prince Aly Khan and Orson Welles – Rita Hayworth

37. John Huston and Artie Shaw – Evelyn Keyes

38. Gene Tierney and Hedy Lamarr – Howard Lee

39. Joan Fontaine and Ida Lupino – Collier Young

40. Joe DiMaggio and Arthur Miller – Marilyn Monroe

41. Gary Oldman and Martin Scorsese – Isabella Rossellini

42. John F. Kennedy and Aristotle Onassis – Jacqueline Onassis

43. Rachel Roberts and Kay Kendall – Sir Rex Harrison

44. Thelma Todd and Gloria Vanderbilt – Pat DiCiccio

45. Dudley Moore and Pinchas Zukerman – Tuesday Weld

46. Jennie Churchill and Mrs Patrick Campbell – George Cornwallis–West

47. Donald Dewar and Lord Alexander Irvine – Alison McNair

48. Stavros Niarchos and Aristotle Onassis – Tina Livanos

49. James Hunt and Richard Burton – Suzy Hunt

50. Paulette Goddard and Oona O'Neill – Charlie Chaplin

51. Sonny Bono and Greg Allman – Cher

52. Peter Sellers and Slim Jim McDonnell – Britt Ekland

53. George Sanders and Conrad Hilton – Zsa Zsa Gabor

54. Fiona Fullerton and Susan George – Simon MacCorkindale

55. Liam Gallagher and Jim Kerr – Patsy Kensit

56. Bill Travers and Denholm Elliott – Virginia McKenna

13 CELEBRITIES WHO MARRIED THEIR MANAGERS

1. Cilla Black

2. Nikki Diamond (Scorpio)

3. Neneh Cherry

4. Joe Bugner

5. Clodagh Rodgers

6. Celine Dion

7. Pam Ayres

8. Charlotte Rampling

9. LaToya Jackson

10. Caron Keating

11. Anthea Turner

12. Jackie Mason

13. Judy Garland

3 CELEBRITIES WHO MARRIED THEIR MINDERS

1. Roseanne Arnold

2. Patty Hearst

3. Princess Stephanie of Monaco

64 CELEBRITIES WHO HAVE NEVER MARRIED

1. Irma Kurtz
2. Sir Edward Heath
3. Terence Stamp
4. Julie Christie
5. Sir Cliff Richard
6. Geoffrey Boycott
7. Valerie Singleton
8. Selina Scott
9. Sir Jimmy Savile
10. Mary Peters
11. Jeremy Paxman
12. Sabrina Guinness
13. Betty Boothroyd
14. Timothy Dalton
15. Celia Hammond
16. Zandra Rhodes
17. Screaming Lord Sutch
18. Russ Conway
19. Oliver Sacks
20. Davina Galica
21. Harold 'Dickie' Bird
22. Celia Imrie
23. Laraine Ashton
24. Gloria Steinem
25. Clare Latimer
26. Ralph Nader
27. Stephanie Lawrence
28. Dame Alicia Markova
29. Lynsey De Paul
30. Joanna David
31. Michael Winner
32. Patricia Routledge
33. Mystic Meg
34. Patrick Moore
35. Jean Alexander
36. Linford Christie
37. Marcelle D'Argy Smith
38. Lindka Cierach
39. Lady Jane Wellesley
40. Celia Brayfield
41. Jerry Brown
42. Robert Stigwood
43. Kate Adie
44. Aaron Copland
45. Eleanor Bron
46. Anne Charleston
47. Diane Keaton
48. Peggy Mount
49. Al Pacino
50. Leonard Cohen
51. Ann Widdecombe
52. Felix Dennis
53. Lionel Bart
54. Nicholas Lyndhurst
55. Annie Leibovitz
56. Nico
57. Cristina Odone
58. Jacqueline Bisset
59. Fanny Ardant
60. Sir Cyril Smith
61. Simone Simon
62. Wilfred Thesiger
63. Anne Gregg
64. Richard Chamberlain

61 DEAD CELEBRITIES WHO NEVER MARRIED

1. Greta Garbo
2. Sir Isaac Newton
3. Florence Nightingale
4. Ludwig van Beethoven
5. Cecil Rhodes
6. Frederic Chopin
7. Dame Flora Robson
8. Queen Elizabeth I
9. Henri de Toulouse-Lautrec
10. Jane Austen
11. Louisa May Alcott
12. Christabel Pankhurst
13. Giacomo Casanova
14. Admiral John Byng
15. Alma Cogan
16. Viscount Tonypandy
17. Alexander Pope
18. Lillian Gish
19. Tommy Nutter
20. P.L. Travers
21. George Gershwin
22. Juan Fangio
23. Tessie O'Shea
24. Dame Gwen Ffrangcon-Davies
25. Henry James
26. Lilian Baylis
27. Arthur Schopenhauer
28. Ronnie Scott
29. Helene Hanff
30. David Hume
31. John Locke
32. Jean-Paul Sartre
33. Rene Descartes
34. Immanuel Kant
35. Friedrich Nietzsche
36. Philip Larkin
37. Patricia Highsmith
38. Adam Smith
39. Baroness Nancy Seear
40. Barry Evans
41. A.L. Rowse
42. Edgar Degas
43. Susan Fleetwood
44. Rory Gallagher
45. Maria Montessori
46. Edward Lear
47. Doris Speed
48. Benny Hill
49. Franco Zeffirelli
50. Stendhal
51. Johannes Brahms
52. Rupert Brooke
53. Voltaire
54. Joan Maynard
55. Mack Sennett
56. Coco Chanel
57. Lord Arnold Goodman
58. Vitas Gerulaitis
59. Stephane Grappelli
60. Frank Richards
61. Ivor Novello

19 CELEBRITY COUPLES WHO REMARRIED EACH OTHER AFTER GETTING DIVORCED

1. Elizabeth Taylor and Richard Burton
2. Melanie Griffith and Don Johnson
3. Sarah Miles and Robert Bolt
4. Elliott Gould and Jenny Bogart
5. Robert Wagner and Natalie Wood
6. Dorothy Parker and Alan Campbell
7. George Peppard and Elizabeth Ashley
8. Jane Wyman and Fred Karger
9. Dionne Warwick and Bill Elliott
10. Paul Hogan and Noelene Edwards
11. Jose Ferrer and Rosemary Clooney
12. George C. Scott and Colleen Dewhurst
13. Owen and Vicki Oyston
14. Asil and Ayesha Nadir
15. Baroness Rendell and Don Rendell
16. Dennis Wilson and Karen Lamm
17. Lucille Ball and Desi Arnaz
18. Milton Berle and Joyce Matthews
19. Billy Rose and Joyce Matthews

3 CELEBRITIES WHO MARRIED NINE TIMES

1. Mike Love
2. Zsa Zsa Gabor
3. Pancho Villa

5 CELEBRITIES WHO MARRIED EIGHT TIMES

1. Marie McDonald

2. Mickey Rooney

3. Alan Jay Lerner

4. Artie Shaw

5. Elizabeth Taylor: (twice to the same man)

8 CELEBRITIES WHO MARRIED SEVEN TIMES

1. Lana Turner

2. Richard Pryor

3. Martha Raye

4. Barbara Hutton

5. Claude Rains

6. Dick Haymes

7. Stan Laurel (three times to the same woman)

8. Jennifer O'Neill

13 CELEBRITIES WHO MARRIED SIX TIMES

1. Sir Rex Harrison
2. Johnny Weissmuller
3. Gloria Swanson
4. Hedy Lamarr
5. Leland Hayward
6. Norman Mailer
7. King Henry VIII
8. Larry King
9. Harold Robbins
10. Steve Earle
11. Jerry Lee Lewis
12. Lionel Stander
13. Tom Mix

33 CELEBRITIES WHO MARRIED FIVE TIMES

1. Stavros Niarchos
2. Gerald Kingsland
3. David Lean
4. Ernest Borgnine
5. Arlene Dahl
6. George C. Scott (twice to the same woman)
7. George Peppard (twice to the same woman)
8. John Huston
9. Vivian Nicholson
10. John Paul Getty II
11. Roy Boulting
12. Hugh Tayfield
13. Ginger Rogers
14. Rue McClanahan
15. Mamie Van Doren
16. Victor Mature
17. Eva Gabor
18. Judy Garland
19. Henry Fonda
20. Jane Wyman (twice to the same man)
21. George Foreman
22. Rita Hayworth
23. Ingmar Bergman
24. Tammy Wynette
25. Clark Gable
26. Veronica Lake
27. Dick Emery
28. George Brent
29. Richard Burton (twice to the same woman)
30. Constance Bennett
31. John Osborne
32. Jane Powell
33. Xavier Cugat

103 CELEBRITIES WHO MARRIED FOUR TIMES

1. Frank Sinatra
2. Joan Collins
3. Jason Robards
4. Ethel Merman
5. Doris Day
6. Jeffrey Bernard
7. Andre Previn
8. Ann Iverson
9. Jim Davidson
10. Terry Moore
11. Merle Oberon
12. Lord Woodrow Wyatt
13. Constance Talmadge
14. Keith Floyd
15. Dennis Hopper
16. Tony Curtis
17. Janet Leigh
18. Ernest Hemingway
19. Rhonda Fleming
20. Barry Humphries
21. Loretta Young
22. Sir Robert Stephens
23. Viveca Lindfors
24. John Derek
25. David Soul
26. Donald Pleasence
27. Danielle Steel
28. Robert Evans
29. Bertrand Russell
30. Betty Hutton
31. Jackie Coogan
32. Myrna Loy
33. Sir Peter Hall
34. Sir Charlie Chaplin
35. George Sanders
36. Bertice Reading
37. Paulette Goddard
38. Peggy Lee
39. Bette Davis
40. Al Jolson
41. Eva Bartok
42. Jane Seymour
43. Bill Waddington
44. Michael Crichton
45. Michael Wilding
46. Anouk Aimee
47. Peter Sellers
48. Lotte Lenya
49. Christina Onassis
50. Jose Ferrer (twice to the same woman)
51. George Balanchine
52. Lawrence Durrell
53. James Cameron (the film director)
54. Kim Philby
55. Yul Brynner
56. Leslie Charteris
57. Bertolt Brecht
58. Lionel Barrymore
59. Melanie Griffith (twice to the same man)
60. Joan Fontaine
61. Gloria Grahame
62. Erica Jong
63. Maxine Audley
64. Gloria Vanderbilt
65. Humphrey Bogart
66. Sandra Howard
67. Cary Grant
68. Margaret Sullavan
69. Sir Freddie Laker
70. Christie Brinkley
71. Barbara Amiel
72. Robert Beatty
73. Madeleine Carroll
74. Jan Leeming
75. Andy McNab
76. Sir Alfred Ayer
77. Joan Crawford (each marriage lasted precisely *four* years!)
78. King Husain of Jordan
79. Joe Papp
80. Bill Edrich
81. Connie Francis
82. Barbara Follett
83. Mao Tse-Tung
84. Lindsay Wagner
85. John Trevelyan
86. Dinah Sheridan
87. Mary Astor
88. Josephine Baker
89. Brigitte Bardot
90. Joan Bennett
91. Dudley Moore
92. Virginia Hill
93. David Bailey
94. Evelyn Keyes
95. Veronica Lake
96. Carole Landis
97. Hattie McDaniel
98. Eddie Fisher
99. Gig Young
100. Miriam Hopkins
101. Charlie Smirke
102. Burgess Meredith
103. Janet Street-Porter

6 CELEBRITY MEN WHO MARRIED OLDER WOMEN

1. Robert Browning (Elizabeth Barrett was six years older than him)
2. Raymond Chandler (Pearl Bowen was 17 years older than him)
3. Clark Gable (both of his first two wives were considerably older than him – his first wife, Josephine Dillon, was 17 years older than him)
4. Benjamin Disraeli (Mary Wyndham Lewis was 12 years older than him)
5. William Shakespeare (Anne Hathaway was seven years older than him)
6. Roger Moore (Dorothy Squires was nine years older than him)

18 CELEBRITY WOMEN WHO MARRIED YOUNGER MEN

1. Sarah Bernhardt (her husband was 11 years her junior)
2. Martha Raye (married a man, Mark Harris, 33 years her junior)
3. Colette (her third husband was 17 years younger than her)
4. Elizabeth Taylor (married Larry Fortensky, who was 20 years her junior)
5. Edith Piaf (married Theo Sarapo who was 20 years her junior)
6. Merle Oberon (married Robert Wolders, who was 25 years her junior)
7. Jennie Churchill (married George Cornwallis-West who was 20 years younger than her and Montagu Porch who was 23 years younger than her)
8. Marti Webb (married Tim Flavin who was 15 years her junior and Tom Button who is 23 years her junior)
9. Arlene Dahl (married Marc Rosen who was 22 years younger than her)
10. Sian Phillips (married Robin Sachs who is 17 years younger than her)
11. Jenny Lind (married Otto Goldschmidt who was nine years her junior)
12. Olivia Newton-John (married Matt Lattanzi who is 11 years younger than her)
13. Kate Jackson (she twice married men who were six years her junior)
14. Joanna Lumley (her husband Stephen Barlow is eight years younger than her)
15. Joan Collins (her fourth husband, Peter Holm, was 14 years her junior)
16. Ruth Gordon (her husband, Garson Kanin, was 16 years her junior)
17. Isadora Duncan (her husband, Sergei Esenin, was 17 years her junior)
18. Janet Street-Porter (her fourth husband, David Solkin, was 22 years her junior)

31 CELEBRITIES WHO MARRIED BEFORE THE AGE OF 17

1. Josephine Baker (13)
2. Loretta Lynn (13)
3. Mahatma Gandhi (13)
4. June Havoc (13)
5. Marie Antoinette (14)
6. Jerry Lee Lewis (14)
7. Janet Leigh (14)
8. Emma Ridley (15)
9. Mary, Queen of Scots (15)
10. Zsa Zsa Gabor (15)
11. Princess Shahnaz Husain (15)
12. Marthe Bibesco (15)
13. Catya Sassoon (15)
14. Princess Ira Von Furstenberg (15)
15. Annie Oakley (15)
16. Jihan Sadat (Mrs Anwar Sadat) (15)
17. Fanny Brice (15)
18. Dolores Del Rio (16)
19. Sophie Tucker (16)
20. Lisa St Aubin De Teran (16)
21. Marti Caine (16)
22. Kay Mellor (16)
23. Placido Domingo (16)
24. Beryl Markham (16)
25. Princess Soraya (16)
26. Marilyn Monroe (16)
27. Raquel Welch (16)
28. Catherine The Great (16)
29. Ellen Terry (16)
30. Beverley Callard (16)
31. Joan Bennett (16)

34 CELEBRITY COUPLES WHO WERE MARRIED IN LAS VEGAS

1. Ursula Andress and John Derek

2. John and Bo Derek

3. Melanie Griffith and Don Johnson (the first time)

4. Samantha Janus and Mauro Mantovani

5. Noel Gallagher and Meg Matthews

6. Sheena Easton and Tim Delarm

7. George Clooney and Talia Balsam (by an Elvis impersonator)

8. Paul Newman and Joanne Woodward

9. Clint Eastwood and Dina Ruiz

10. Paula Yates and Bob Geldof

11. Caroline Aherne and Peter Hook

12. Jason Connery and Mia Sara

13. Ruby Wax and Trevor Walton

14. Frank Sinatra and Mia Farrow

15. Natasha Henstridge and Damian Chapa

16. Ross Boatman and Sophie Camara

17. Emma Ridley and Robert Pereno

18. Michael Caine and Shakira Baksh

19. Nicolas Cage and Patricia Arquette (fittingly, for a man who won an Oscar for *Leaving Las Vegas*)

20. Joan Collins and Peter Holm

21. Richard Gere and Cindy Crawford

22. Demi Moore and Bruce Willis

23. Caroline Goodall and Derek Hoxby

24. Dinah Sheridan and Aubrey Ison

25. Gabriel Byrne and Ellen Barkin

26. Sylvia Kristel and Alan Turner

27. Dudley Moore and Brogan Lane

28. Elvis Presley and Priscilla Beaulieu (*not* by an Elvis impersonator)

29. Jonathan Ross and Jane Goldman

30. Richard and Sally Burton

31. Brigitte Bardot and Gunther Sachs

32. Jane Russell and Robert Waterfield

33. Four of Mickey Rooney's weddings took place in Las Vegas. Maybe he got a bulk purchase discount.

34. Milla Jovovich and Luc Besson

12 CELEBRITY WOMEN WHO POPPED THE QUESTION

1. Zsa Zsa Gabor. The much married actress proposed to her first husband when she was just 15 years old. He accepted and they married before her 16th birthday. 'Dahlink' Zsa Zsa had recently been disqualified from the Miss Hungary title for being under 16.

2. Pamela Stephenson. The comedienne and the comedian, Billy Connolly, lived together and had three children before deciding to tie the knot. During that time, she has said that they ". . . went through periods of proposing to each other".

3. Countess Spencer. The former model proposed to the Princess of Wales's brother in the days when he was plain Viscount Althorp. Apparently, he asked her to marry him but she wouldn't answer because she thought he might be tiddly. She asked him the next morning.

4. Joan Collins. The actress (and novelist) proposed to Anthony Newley after deciding that he was the man for her. They had both been married before and their marriage broke up too but they have remained friends.

5. Queen Victoria. Victoria became Queen of England at the age of 18 and quickly realised that she had an obligation to produce an heir, so she decided to marry her German cousin, Prince Albert. She duly summoned him and proposed marriage, telling him that it would make her 'too happy' if he would accept.

6. Jerry Hall. 13 years before they tied the knot, the Bovril-drinking Texan-born model had given Mick Jagger an ultimatum that they had to get married within ten years. The three years' grace obviously helped to concentrate the Rolling Stone's mind.

7. Edwina Currie. Of all the women in this list – even including the two Queens – the former MP is the least surprising. She has said of her husband that she ". . . found out he was very close to his parents" and so ". . . asked him to marry me".

8. Janet Brown. The comedienne and impressionist has said that instead of her intended asking for her "hand in marriage", it was '. . . the other way round'.

9. Queen Elizabeth II. Although no one has ever been told whether the Queen proposed to Philip or whether he proposed to her, it is thought likely that she was the one who popped the question as royal protocol demanded it.

10. Maureen Lipman. The *Agony* actress proposed to husband Jack Rosenthal, the playwright and former *Coronation Street* writer. He had been married before and she says that it took her four years to persuade him to tie the knot.

11. Judy Cornwell. When the *Keeping Up Appearances* actress and bestselling novelist met John Parry, it was love at first sight. Nevertheless, she was the one to pop the question.

12. Daryl Hannah. The actress met Mark Halperin in 1980 and proposed to him almost immediately. They were married in Mexico just two days after they met (although there are doubts whether the marriage was actually registered).

65 CELEBRITY ENGAGEMENTS WHICH DIDN'T LEAD TO MARRIAGE

(Note: In these informal times, what is and what isn't an engagement can sometimes be a moot point – especially after the relationship has ended. A jilted boyfriend of someone who has gone on to become famous tells the press that they were engaged to be married and who can gainsay him? In the good old days, all engage-ments were announced in *The Times* and everyone knew where they stood. Nowadays, with couples much more likely to cohabit before marriage, the word 'fiancée' is used as a less formal synonym for 'co-habitee'.

1. Audrey Hepburn and Lord James Hanson
2. Michelle Pfeiffer and Fisher Stevens
3. Ronan Keating and Vernie Bennett
4. Jimmy Connors and Chris Evert
5. Sophie Anderton and Simon Rubel
6. Lauren Bacall and Frank Sinatra
7. Fred Couples and Tawnya Dodd
8. Lord James Hanson and Evelyn Diane Bates
9. Sinitta and Thomas Arklie
10. Nicholas Lyndhurst and Gail Parr
11. Abraham Lincoln and Mary Todd
12. James Hewitt and Emma Stewardson
13. Carole Landis and Busby Berkeley
14. Julia Roberts and Kiefer Sutherland
15. Sir David Frost and Diahann Carroll
16. Sir David Frost and Karen Graham
17. Lucille Ball and Broderick Crawford
18. Tessa Dahl and Angus Gibson
19. Steve Wyatt and Dorice Valle Risso (the engagement ended the day before the wedding)
20. Emma Samms and Marvin Hamlisch
21. King George V (when he was Duke of York) and the Honourable Julia Stonor (because she was a Catholic)
22. Princess Stephanie of Monaco and Jean-Yves LeFur
23. James Hewitt and Anna Ferretti
24. Charlie Sheen and Ginger Lynn Allen
25. Jonathan Cake and Olivia Williams
26. Normandie Keith and Lucas White
27. Nicole Appleton and Darren Brodin
28. Naomi Campbell and Adam Clayton
29. Brad Pitt and Gwyneth Paltrow

30. Dodi Fayed and Kelly Fisher

31. David Coulthard and Andrea Murray

32. Greta Garbo and John Gilbert (the engagement ended on the wedding day – she stood him up at the altar)

33. Victoria Adams and Mark Wood

34. Sir Paul McCartney and Jane Asher

35. Brian Cox and Irina Brook

36. Sharon Stone and Michael Benasra

37. Tamara Beckwith and Michael Stone (Sharon's brother)

38. Yasmin Bleeth and Ricky Paul Goldin

39. Claudia Schiffer and David Copperfield

40. Martine McCutcheon and Gareth Cooke

41. Van Morrison and Michelle Rocca

42. Olivia Newton-John and Bruce Welch

43. Thomas Muster and Mariella Theiner

44. Letitia Dean and Martin Ballis

45. Shane Richie and Dawn Rodger

46. Dervla Kirwan and Robert Caldwell

47. Brian Harvey and Daniella Westbrook

48. Stan Collymore and Lotta Farley

49. Samantha Fox and Peter Foster

50. Walter Swinburn and Britt Eldrup

51. Shannen Doherty and Dean Jay Factor

52. Tania Bryer and Count Gianfranco Cicogna

53. James Gilbey and Lady Alethea Savile

54. Phil Tufnell and Jane McEvoy

55. Sharon Stone and Bill McDonald

56. Johnny Depp and Winona Ryder

57. Liza Minnelli and Desi Arnaz Junior

58. Bobby Davro and Zoe Nicholas

59. Axl Rose and Stephanie Seymour

60. Julie Goodyear and Jack Diamond

61. John Daly and Bettye Fulford

62. Roger Vadim and Catherine Deneuve

63. Bryan Ferry and Jerry Hall

64. Cheryl Baker and Martin Wood

65. Neil Morrissey and Elizabeth Carling

8 CELEBRITY MARRIAGE PROPOSALS WHICH WERE TURNED DOWN

1. Ernest Hemingway's proposal to Gertrude Stein
2. Duke of Westminster's proposal to Coco Chanel
3. Howard Hughes's proposal to Susan Hayward
4. James Orr's proposal to Farrah Fawcett
5. The Earl of Aylesford's proposal to M.M. Kaye
6. Madonna's proposal to Dennis Rodman (three times!)
7. Dodi Fayed's proposal to Traci Lind
8. James Stewart's proposal to Olivia de Havilland

2 CELEBRITIES WHO MARRIED LATE FOR THE FIRST TIME

1. W. B. Yeats – 52
2. Sir Leon Brittan – 41

20 CELEBRITIES WHO WERE VIRGINS ON THEIR WEDDING DAY

1. Victor Hugo (did it nine times on his wedding night)
2. Elizabeth Taylor
3. Gwen Taylor
4. Priscilla Presley
5. Marthe Bibesco
6. Tiny Tim
7. Jonathan Edwards
8. Marjorie Proops
9. Gloria Hunniford
10. Lord Laurence Olivier
11. Ava Gardner
12. Loretta Lynn
13. Raquel Welch
14. Catherine the Great
15. William Gladstone
16. Dorothy Dandridge
17. Mark Twain
18. Vivien Leigh
19. Terry Moore
20. Gloria Swanson

6 CELEBRITY COUPLES WHO DIDN'T HAVE SEX ON THEIR WEDDING NIGHTS

1. Elizabeth Taylor and Nicky Hilton. (She was a virgin when they married but they didn't actually have sex until their third night of marriage)
2. Richard Gere and Cindy Crawford
3. Samantha Janus and Mauro Mantovani
4. Brian Aherne and Joan Fontaine
5. Liza Minnelli and Peter Allen
6. Walt Disney and Lillian Bounds (Walt had toothache)

45 CELEBRITY MARRIAGES WHICH TRULY LASTED (*still going in 1998)

1. Lord Longford and Elizabeth, Countess of Longford (67 years*)
2. Perry and Roselle Como (65 years*)
3. Sir Donald and Lady Jessie Bradman (65 years)
4. Anthony and Lady Violet Powell (64 years*)
5. Bob and Dolores Hope (64 years*)
6. James and Frances Cagney (63 years)
7. Sir Alec and Lady Merula Guinness (60 years*)
8. Karl and Mona Malden (60 years*)
9. Fred Zinnemann and Renee Bartlett (60 years)
10. Michael Denison and Dulcie Gray (59 years*)
11. Mary and Ernest Whitehouse (58 years*)
12. Jack and Florence Haley (58 years)
13. Dame Thora Hird and Jimmy Scott (58 years)
14. Sir John Mills and Mary Hayley Bell (57 years*)
15. The Duke and Duchess of Devonshire (57 years*)
16. Sir Matt and Lady Jean Busby (57 years)
17. Ray and Gwendolyn Bolger (57 years)
18. Max and Gladys Bygraves (56 years*)
19. Professor Richard and Mary Hoggart (56 years*)
20. Lord and Lady Peter Carrington (56 years*)
21. Lord and Lady Lew Grade (56 years*)
22. Charlton and Lydia Heston (54 years*)
23. Sir Ian and Sybil MacGregor (54 years)
24. Lord and Lady Denis Healey (53 years*)
25. Lord Richard Attenborough and Sheila Sim (53 years*)
26. Lord Brabourne and Lady Mountbatten (52 years*)
27. Robin and Patricia Bailey (52 years)
28. Walter and Ruth Pidgeon (52 years)
29. Hume Cronyn and Jessica Tandy (52 years)
30. Pat and Eloise O'Brien (52 years)
31. Carl and Emma Jung (52 years)
32. Queen Elizabeth II and Prince Philip (51 years*)
33. Dick and Mary Francis (51 years*)
34. Lord and Lady Yehudi Menuhin (51 years*)
35. The Rev W. and Margaret Awdry (51 years)
36. Sir Harry and Lady Myra Secombe (50 years*)
37. Googie Withers and John McCallum (50 years*)
38. Federico Fellini and Gulietta Masina (50 years)
39. Marlene Dietrich and Rudolf Sieber (50 years)
40. Dick and Marjorie Van Dyke (49 years*)
41. Michael Foot and Jill Craigie (49 years*)
42. Eli and Anne Wallach (49 years*)
43. Joyce and Reggie Grenfell (49 years – she died two weeks before their golden wedding anniversary)
44. Jackie and Sunnie Mann (49 years – she died some six months before their golden wedding anniversary)
45. Lord James and Audrey Callaghan (60 years*)

56 CELEBRITY MARRIAGES WHICH DIDN'T LAST

Marriages which broke up as a result of death have been omitted. Please note also that durations are approximate and refer either to the time the couple separated or divorced.

1. Giuseppe Garibaldi and Giuseppina Raimondi (less than one day)

2. Rudolph Valentino and Jean Acker (one day)

3. Adolf Hitler and Eva Braun (one day. I know death ended this marriage but it was suicide, i.e. it was their decision)

4. Jean Arthur and Julian Anker (one day)

5. Julie Goodyear and Tony Rudman (one day – he walked out on her during the wedding reception saying that he didn't like the idea of living in the spotlight)

6. Katherine Mansfield and George Mansfield (one day)

7. Robin Givens and Svetozar Marinkovic (one day)

8. Fanny Brice and Frank White (three days)

9. John Heard and Margot Kidder (six days)

10. Dennis Hopper and Michelle Phillips (one week)

11. Patty Duke and Michael Tell (two weeks)

12. Carole Landis and Irving Wheeler (three weeks)

13. Germaine Greer and Paul Du Feu (three weeks)

14. Katharine Hepburn and Ludlow Ogden Smith (three weeks)

15. Shannen Doherty and Ashley Hamilton (three weeks)

16. Gloria Swanson and Wallace Beery (three weeks)

17. Ethel Merman and Ernest Borgnine (three weeks)

18. Burt Lancaster and June Ernst (less than one month)

19. John Milton and Mary Powell (one month)

20. Jane Wyman and Eugene Wyman (one month)

21. Greer Garson and Edward Snelson (five weeks)

22. George Brent and Constance Worth (five weeks)

23. Jean Peters and Stuart Cramer (five weeks)

24. Peter De Savary and Alice Simms (six weeks)

25. Drew Barrymore and Jeremy Thomas (six weeks)

26. Derek Fowlds and Lesley Judd (two months)

27. Ashley Hamilton and Angie Evehardt (68 days)

28. Frank Lloyd Wright and Miriam Noel (three months)

29. Leslie Ash and Jonathan Weston (three months)

30. Tracy Edwards and Simon Lawrence (three months)

31. Joanna Lumley and Jeremy Lloyd (four months)

32. Marco Pierre White and Lisa Butcher (four months)

33. Sylvia Kristel and Alan Turner (five months)

34. Charlie Sheen and Donna Peele (five months)

35. Carole Landis and Willie Hunts Jr (five months)

36. Fanny Cradock and Arthur Chapman (a few months)

37. Elton John and Renate Blauel (a few months)

38. Don Johnson and Melanie Griffith (first time around – a few months)

39. Arthur C Clarke and Marilyn Mayfield (six months)

40. Christie Brinkley and Ricky Taubman (seven months)

41. Dennis Wilson and Karen Lamm (seven months first time around; two weeks second time around)

42. Jean Harlow and Hal Rosson (eight months)

43. Kelsey and Leanne Grammer (eight months)

44. Dodi Fayed and Suzanne Gregard (eight months)

45. Emma Samms and Bansi Nagji (eight months)

46. Judy Garland and David Rose (eight months)

47. Marilyn Monroe and Joe DiMaggio (nine months)

48. Fiona Wright and Mark Chattwell (nine months)

49. Sheena and Sandi Easton (nine months)

50. Jim Carrey and Lauren Holly (ten months)

51. Ellen Terry and George Watts (ten months)

52. Jim Davidson and Sue Walpole (eleven months)

53. Sarah Bernhardt and Aristides Damala (less than a year)

54. Whoopi Goldberg and Dave Claessen (less than a year)

55. Julie Goodyear and Richard Skrob (one year)

56. Pat Phoenix and Peter Marsh (one year)

5 CELEBRITY POLYGAMISTS

1. King Solomon
2. King David
3. Brigham Young
4. Nero
5. Joseph Smith

16 CELEBRITIES WITH FAMOUS FATHERS-IN-LAW

1. Gregor Fisher – Peter Vaughan
2. Woody Allen – Andre Previn
3. Jonny Lee Miller – Jon Voight
4. Barry Humphries – Sir Stephen Spender
5. Loyd Grossman – Sir David Puttnam
6. Anthony Quinn – Cecil B. De Mille
7. Axl Rose – Don Everly
8. Charles Chaplin – Eugene O'Neill
9. Karen Dotrice – Wilfred Hyde-White
10. Richard Wagner – Franz Liszt
11. Belinda Carlisle – James Mason
12. Sir David Frost – The Duke of Norfolk
13. John McEnroe – Ryan O'Neal
14. Vincent Hanna – Lord Gerry Fitt
15. W. Somerset Maugham – Dr Barnardo
16. Shannen Doherty – George Hamilton

4 CELEBRITIES WHO MARRIED THEIR SPOUSE'S RELATIONS

1. Cleopatra married the brothers Ptolemy XIII and then when he died Ptolemy XIV.
2. George Sanders married the Gabor sisters, Zsa Zsa and Magda.
3. Barbara Cartland married the McCorquodale cousins
4. Gloria Grahame's second husband was the film director Nicholas Ray. Her fourth husband was his son, Tony

15 CELEBRITIES WHO WERE NAMED AS 'CO-RESPONDENT' IN DIVORCE PETITIONS

1. Warren Beatty (in the divorce of Sir Peter Hall and Leslie Caron)
2. Earl Spencer (Don and Chantal Collopy)
3. Mick Jagger (Marianne Faithfull and John Dunbar)
4. Anthony Booth (David Elliott and Stephenie Buckley)
5. George Weidenfeld (Cyril Connolly and Barbara Skelton)
6. Cyril Connolly (George Weidenfeld and Barbara Skelton – this was the order in which this remarkable true-life soap occurred)
7. James Hewitt (David and Sally Faber)
8. Olivia Newton-John (Bruce and Ann Welch)
9. Jessie Matthews (Evelyn Laye and Sonnie Hale)
10. John Osborne (Dr Roger and Penelope Gilliatt)
11. Dorothy Squires (Roger Moore and Doorn van Steyn)
12. Georgie Fame (The Marquess and Marchioness of Londonderry)
13. Glenn Hoddle (Jeffrey and Vanessa Shean)
14. W. Somerset Maugham (Henry and Syrie Wellcome)
15. Ross Kemp (Lucien Taylor and Helen Patrick)

14 BRITISH PRIME MINISTERS WHO COMMITTED ADULTERY

1. David Lloyd George
2. Lord John Russell
3. Lord Grey
4. George Canning
5. The Duke of Devonshire
6. The Duke of Wellington
7. Lord Palmerston
8. Benjamin Disraeli
9. Lord Melbourne
10. Sir Robert Walpole
11. The Duke of Grafton
12. The Earl of Bute
13. Ramsay MacDonald
14. Herbert Asquith

Hollywood & Royal Romantic Liaisons

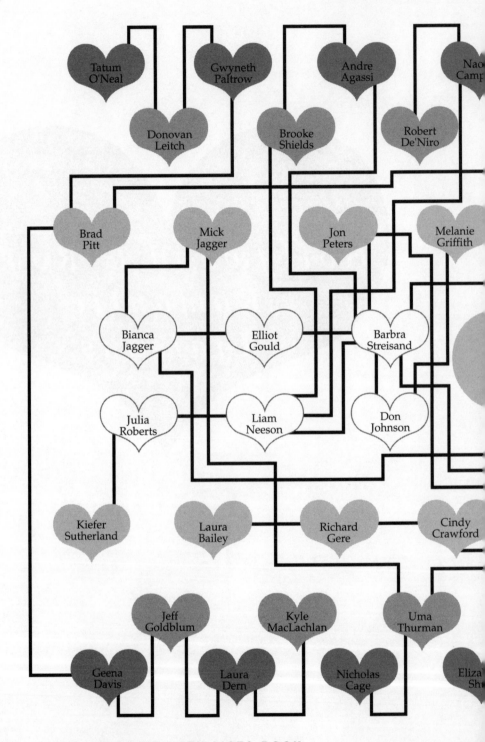

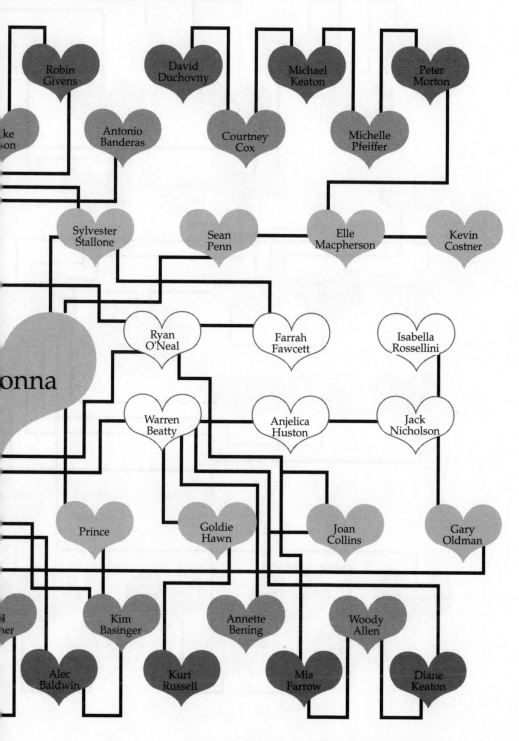

Robin Givens

David Duchovny

Michael Keaton

Peter Morton

ke on

Antonio Banderas

Courtney Cox

Michelle Pfeiffer

Sylvester Stallone

Sean Penn

Elle Macpherson

Kevin Costner

Ryan O'Neal

Farrah Fawcett

Isabella Rossellini

onna

Warren Beatty

Anjelica Huston

Jack Nicholson

Prince

Goldie Hawn

Joan Collins

Gary Oldman

Kim Basinger

Annette Bening

Woody Allen

er

Alec Baldwin

Kurt Russell

Mia Farrow

Diane Keaton

Martin Amis
Novelist

Mick Imlah
Journalist

Emmanuel Olympitis
Company Chairman

Mick Jagger
Singer

Isobel Fonseca
Novelist

Emily Todhunter
Interior Designer

Jack Nicholson
Actor

Princess Anne
Royal

Rosemary Pitman
Socialite

Lady Jane Wellesley
Heiress

Richard Parker Bowles
Socialite

Lucia Santa Cruz
Ambassador's daughter

Sabrina Guinness
TV execut

Lady Victoria Percy
Aristocrat

Lady Caroline Percy
Aristocrat

Andrew Parker Bowles
Retired Officer

Charl Princ

Camilla Parker Bowles
Royal mistress

Anna Wallace
Socialite

Laura Jo Watkins
Admiral's daughter

Carolyn Benson
Party organiser

Fiona Fullerton
Actress

Simon McCorkindale
Actor

Susan George
Actress

Lady Jane Grosvenor
Heiress

LadySarah Spencer
Aristocrat

Amand Knatchb
Aristocr

Davinia Sheffield
Aristocrat

Marco Pierre White
Chef

Gabriel Donoso
Polo player

Fergus Greer
Photographer

Jack Jones
Singer

Lisa Butcher
Model

Caroline Aherne
Comedienne

Liaisons

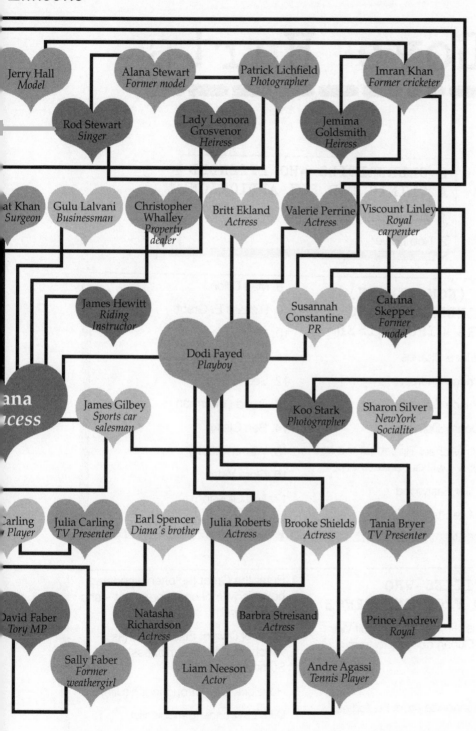

Jerry Hall
Model

Alana Stewart
Former model

Patrick Lichfield
Photographer

Imran Khan
Former cricketer

Rod Stewart
Singer

Lady Leonora
Grosvenor
Heiress

Jemima
Goldsmith
Heiress

at Khan
Surgeon

Gulu Lalvani
Businessman

Christopher
Whalley
*Property
dealer*

Britt Ekland
Actress

Valerie Perrine
Actress

Viscount Linley
*Royal
carpenter*

James Hewitt
*Riding
Instructor*

Susannah
Constantine
PR

Catrina
Skepper
*Former
model*

Dodi Fayed
Playboy

ana
cess

James Gilbey
*Sports car
salesman*

Koo Stark
Photographer

Sharon Silver
*New York
Socialite*

Carling
Player

Julia Carling
TV Presenter

Earl Spencer
Diana's brother

Julia Roberts
Actress

Brooke Shields
Actress

Tania Bryer
TV Presenter

David Faber
Tory MP

Natasha
Richardson
Actress

Barbra Streisand
Actress

Prince Andrew
Royal

Sally Faber
*Former
weathergirl*

Liam Neeson
Actor

Andre Agassi
Tennis Player

Chapter 6

Love Hurts

2 CELEBRITIES WHO ATTENDED A CLINIC FOR SEX ADDICTION

1. Michael Douglas
2. Rob Lowe

18 (NON-JEWISH) CELEBRITIES WHO WERE CIRCUMCISED

1. Prince Charles
2. Prince Andrew
3. Prince Edward
4. Donny Osmond
5. Sir Michael Tippett (at the age of 5 – without anaesthetic)
6. Clint Eastwood
7. Mike Stroud
8. Matt Dillon
9. Richard E. Grant
10. Mick Jagger
11. David Bailey
12. Sean Penn
13. David Letterman
14. Ben Clarke
15. Warren Beatty
16. Gore Vidal
17. Mel Gibson
18. Tom Cruise

7 CELEBRITIES WHO SUFFERED FROM IMPOTENCE

1. Saddam Hussain (before the Gulf War – he flew in Cuban doctors to treat him)
2. J.M. Barrie
3. Napoleon Bonaparte (from his forties onwards)
4. Peter the Great (he often wondered how his wife became pregnant – she took lovers)
5. General Dwight Eisenhower (as vouchsafed by his 'mistress', Kay Summersby)
6. Havelock Ellis (throughout his life)
7. D.H. Lawrence (periodically)

27 OTHER CELEBRITIES WHO CONTRACTED VENEREAL DISEASES

1. Abraham
2. David
3. Job
4. Julius Caesar
5. King Herod
6. Emperor Tiberius
7. Charlemagne
8. Charles V of France
9. Charles VIII of France
10. John of Gaunt
11. Pope Alexander VI
12. Pope Julius II
13. Pope Leo X
14. Erasmus
15. Cardinal Thomas Wolsey
16. John F. Kennedy
17. Cardinal Richelieu
18. Casanova
19. James Boswell. He died from the effects of gonorrhoea
20. Ferdinand Magellan
21. Adolf Hitler
22. August Strindberg
23. Lord Byron. He called his gonorrhoea 'the curse of Venus'
24. Frederic Chopin
25. W. Somerset Maugham
26. Mao Tse-Tung
27. Benvenuto Cellini

1 CELEBRITY WHOSE MARRIAGE TO A JEW PROMPTED THE NAZIS TO ATTEMPT TO POISON HER

1. Josephine Baker. Hermann Goering invited her to dinner and made her eat fish laced with cyanide. Fortunately, members of the French Resistance later arranged for her to have her stomach pumped out.

6 CELEBRITIES WHO CHANGED SEX

1. April Ashley
2. Renee Richards
3. Jan Morris
4. Wendy Carlos
5. Tula
6. Dana International

9 CELEBRITIES WHO SUFFERED FROM PREMATURE EJACULATION

1. King Edward VIII
2. John Maynard Keynes
3. Tony Curtis (in his youth)
4. Havelock Ellis (until the age of 60 and without ever achieving vaginal penetration)
5. Johann Von Goethe (until his late 30s)
6. Groucho Marx (all his life)
7. Henry Fonda (according to ex-wife Margaret Sullavan)
8. Rock Hudson (according to a woman he had sex with)
9. John F. Kennedy

35 CELEBRITIES WHO HAD SYPHILIS

1. Oscar Wilde. He caught it rom a prostitute whilst at university
2. Niccolo Paganini, reduced him to a walking corpse with halitosis and teeth held in with string
3. Al Capone. He caught it in a Brooklyn brothel and it completely changed his personality
4. Bram Stoker. Led to the tertiary stage of syphilis, General Paralysis of The Insane
5. Howard Hughes. He caught it as a young man and it led to his eventual mental and physical decline
6. Paul Gauguin. It eventually killed him
7. King Henry VIII. It eventually killed him
8. Ivan the Terrible. It made him live up to his name
9. Franz Schubert. He died from it
10. Karen Blixen. She died from it
11. Friedrich Nietzsche. He died from it
12. Vincent Van Gogh. The mercury used to treat it destroyed his brain
13. Robert Schumann
14. Bedrich Smetana
15. Guy de Maupassant. It eventually killed him
16. Charles Baudelaire
17. Henri de Toulouse-Lautrec. It combined with alcoholic poisoning to kill him
18. Alexander Dumas Senior. It eventually killed him
19. James Joyce
20. Lola Montez. It made her bald
21. Benito Mussolini. It probably accounted for his megalomania
22. Arthur Schopenhauer
23. Paul Verlaine
24. Groucho Marx
25. Lord Randolph Churchill. It caused him to go mad
26. Ludwig Von Beethoven
27. Cleopatra
28. Christopher Columbus
29. Captain James Cook
30. Johann Von Goethe
31. Francisco Goya
32. Heinrich Heine
33. John Keats
34. Jonathan Swift
35. Franz Schubert

7 CELEBRITIES WHO WROTE PORNOGRAPHY/EROTICA

1. Alexander Dumas Senior (sent his younger lovers dirty poems)
2. Alistair Campbell (wrote features for *Penthouse*)
3. Lynn Barber (wrote features for *Penthouse)*
4. William Faulkner (wrote erotic poems)
5. Adolf Hitler (drew pornographic pictures)
6. Mark Twain (wrote obscene stories and poems)
7. Mystic Meg (wrote sexy stories for *Club International*)

15 CELEBRITY MEN WHO HAD SEX WITH UNDERAGE GIRLS

1. Mark Twain

2. Samuel Pepys

3. Paul Gauguin married (at different times) *three* 14-year old girls

4. Sir Charles Chaplin ("the younger the better")

5. Emile Zola (never actually did anything, but in his middle-age, he certainly fantasized about pre-pubescent girls)

6. Bill Wyman (first had sex with Mandy Smith when she was 13)

7. John Barrymore

8. Casanova (liked seducing teenage virgins)

9. Elvis Presley

10. Terry Coldwell (East 17 musician had sex with a 14-year old girl in 1997)

11. Howard Hughes

12. Marquis de Sade

13. Errol Flynn

14. Fedor Dostoevsky

15. Roman Polanski (at the time of writing, Polanski was still on the run after being charged in 1977 with having unlawful sexual intercourse with a 13-year old girl)

8 CELEBRITIES WHO DIED DURING SEX

1. Pope John XII (beaten to death by the husband of the woman he was making love to)

2. Pope Leo VIII (became paralysed and died whilst having sex with a married woman)

3. Stephen Milligan MP (died of self-asphyxiation)

4. Felix Faure (nineteenth century French President – with a French prostitute)

5. Attila The Hun (On his wedding night. But don't feel sorry for him – it was his twelfth marriage)

6. Lord Palmerston (Having sex with one of his servants on a billiard table.

7. Nelson Rockefeller (having sex with his mistress. Presumably, his wife wasn't happy about this . . .)

8. Pope Paul II (died of a heart attack while being buggered)

53
CELEBRITIES AND THE CELEBRITIES THEY TURNED DOWN

1. Marianne Faithfull turned down Bob Dylan

2. Marianne Faithfull turned down Jimi Hendrix

3. Marlon Brando turned down Tallulah Bankhead

4. Carol White turned down James Caan

5. Anna Ford turned down Peter Jay

6. Olivia de Havilland turned down Errol Flynn

7. Olivia de Havilland turned down Leslie Howard

8. Marlene Dietrich turned down Ernest Hemingway

9. Marlene Dietrich turned down Adolf Hitler (after approaches to her were made by Goebbels and Von Ribbentrop on his behalf)

10. Britt Ekland turned down Ron Ely

11. Ida Lupino turned down Errol Flynn

12. Ava Gardner turned down Howard Hughes

13. Mary Pickford turned down Clark Gable

14. Greta Garbo turned down Aristotle Onassis

15. Evelyn Keyes turned down Harry Cohn

16. Katharine Hepburn turned down Douglas Fairbanks Jr

17. Katharine Hepburn turned down John Barrymore

18. Jean Simmons turned down John F. Kennedy

19. Veronica Lake turned down Errol Flynn

20. Angela Baddeley turned down Lord Laurence Olivier

21. Lord Laurence Olivier turned down Merle Oberon

22. Joan Collins turned down Daryl F. Zanuck

23. Annette Andre turned down Benny Hill

24. Liam Gallagher turned down Paula Yates

25. Tallulah Bankhead turned down John Barrymore

26. Jean Harlow turned down Louis B Mayer

27. Clara Bow turned down Al Jolson

28. Zizi Jeanmaire turned down Howard Hughes (this was after he'd bought over the entire ballet company for a film – purely to seduce her)

29. Gina Lollobrigida turned down Howard Hughes

30. Vaslav Nijinsky turned down Isadora Duncan

31. Gertrude Stein turned down Ernest Hemingway

32. Ava Gardner turned down George C. Scott

33. Jaclyn Smith turned down Warren Beatty

34. Joan Collins turned down Richard Burton

35. Bette Davis turned down Barbara Stanwyck

36. Bette Davis turned down Joan Crawford (according to Hollywood legend – although their lifelong enmity is equally likely to be due to the fact that Davis had an affair with Franchot Tone while he was married to Crawford)

37. Marilyn Monroe turned down Joan Crawford

38. Anthony Perkins turned down Ingrid Bergman

39. Jacqueline Susann turned down Coco Chanel

40. Rita Hayworth turned down Harry Cohn

41. Bette Davis turned down Miriam Hopkins

42. Merle Oberon turned down Stewart Granger

43. Janet Leigh turned down Howard Hughes

44. Marlon Brando turned down Anna Magnani

45. Burt Lancaster turned down Anna Magnani

46. Tyrone Power turned down Norma Shearer

47. Jean Simmons turned down Howard Hughes

48. Grace Kelly turned down Bing Crosby

49. Paul McCartney turned down Little Richard

50. Mrs Patrick Campbell turned down George Bernard Shaw

51. John Wayne turned down Marlene Dietrich

52. Suggs turned down Madonna

53. Hugh Grant turned down Madonna

11 CELEBRITIES WHO COLLECTED PORNOGRAPHY/ EROTICA

1. David Baddiel
2. King Farouk I
3. William Gladstone
4. Adolf Hitler
5. J. Edgar Hoover
6. Samuel Pepys
7. Frederick West
8. A.E. Housman
9. Ian Fleming
10. Philip Larkin
11. Peter Cook

28 CELEBRITY SEX SCANDALS

1. King Edward VII. When he was Prince of Wales, Bertie (as he was known) was a rake. He was forever hopping in and out of beds, usually, married women's beds. Everyone was terribly discreet about all this except when he cuckolded one husband too many and was obliged to go into open court and swear on oath that he *hadn't* had an adulterous relationship with Lady Harriet Mordaunt. Obviously he was lying, but in those days the reputation of the Royal Family was worth more than a Prince's immortal soul.

2. Herbert Asquith. In 1915, the Prime Minister fell for 25-year-old Venetia Stanley. It wasn't reported at the time, but many historians believe that it helped to set the Liberal Party on the road to decline.

3. Errol Flynn. In 1942, the Hollywood star was charged with the statutory rape of Betty Hansen and Peggy Satterlee. He got off but the expression 'in like Flynn' soon became a popular saying.

4. Horatio, Lord Nelson. The openness with which he conducted his love affair with Lady Emma Hamilton shocked all of England and led to King George III ostracizing him.

5. Marie Curie. The great physicist was embroiled in a scandal when she fell in love with Paul Langevin and was accused by Langevin's already estranged wife of "husband stealing". Marie Curie's love letters were published in the newspapers and she received death threats from a French public furious at this Polish woman 'stealing' a French woman's husband.

6. Jeremy Thorpe. The Liberal Party leader was brought to his knees (maybe literally) by 'male model' Norman Scott.

7. Jim Bakker. In 1987, the TV evangelist was brought down by the revelation that he'd had an affair with Jessica Hahn six years earlier.

8. Jimmy Swaggart. In 1987, it was revealed that the TV evangelist was seeing a prostitute. Apparently, they didn't have sex, but she would pose naked while he talked about "perverted" things. In 1991, he was obliged to quit after going with a prostitute.

9. John Profumo. In 1963, the War Minister was obliged to resign after it was discovered that he'd lied to the House of Commons about his affair with Christine Keeler (who was also seeing a Russian agent). This became the yardstick by which all subsequent political sex scandals would be judged.

10. Lord Lambton. In 1973, the Tory Minister for Defence resigned after his affair with call girl Norma Levy was revealed. A few days later, Earl Jellicoe quit as Lord Privy Seal after it was revealed that he too had been with prostitutes.

11. David Mellor. The Tory MP was obliged to quit as Secretary of State for National Heritage in 1992 after his affair with Antonia de Sancha was revealed.

12. Tim Yeo. The Tory MP was obliged to resign as a Minister after it was revealed in December 1993 that he had fathered a child by a woman who wasn't his wife.

13. Richard Spring. The Tory MP resigned as a PPS in 1995 after allegations of a "three-in-a-bed romp".

14. Paddy Ashdown. The Liberal Democrats leader actually found his popularity increasing when it was revealed in 1992 that he once had an affair with his secretary, Patricia Howard.

15. Bill Clinton. It's hard to know where to start. Suffice it to say that Slick Willie's idea of a running mate is to shout, "Quick, Gennifer, they're after us".

16. Michael Jackson. No one (but he himself and the boys involved) knows exactly what happened with the rock star and his 'young friends'. My own instinct is that he's an immature man who enjoys the innocent company of boys, but one has to balance that against a £21 million settlement he made on 14-year-old Jordy Chandler.

17. Gary Hart. In 1984, the senator saw his hopes of becoming President scuppered after his adulterous relationship with Donna Rice came to light. It did however give rise to a wonderful (possibly apocryphal) line from an American (female) voter who said in 1988, "My heart is for Bush but my Bush is for Hart".

18. Robin Cook. In 1997 it was revealed that the new Foreign Secretary was having an affair with his secretary, Gaynor Regan. He dumped his wife and in 1998 married his mistress *while wearing an anorak!* If this is how boring Labour 'scandals' are going to be then bring back the Tories.

19. Rupert Pennant-Rea. In 1995, he resigned as Deputy Governor of the Bank of England after having an affair with Mary Ellen Synon, which included a tryst in the Governor's dressing-room.

20. Sir Allan Green. In 1991, he was obliged to resign as the Director of Public Prosecutions after he was caught kerb crawling in Kings Cross.

21. Jerry Hayes. In 1997, just before the General Election, it was alleged that he'd had a gay affair with Paul Stone, his former researcher. His constituency party stood by him but he lost his seat (although it has to be said that Tory MPs with bigger majorities than his lost theirs too).

22. Major Ronald Ferguson. In 1993, it was revealed that the Duchess of York's father had had an affair with "polo girl" Lesley Player.

23. Frank Bough. In 1988, the doyen of British broadcasters attended 'sex and drugs' parties. In 1992, he was caught visiting a 'sado-masochistic vice den'. "I have been exceedingly stupid", he was quoted as having said.

24. Christopher Trace. The first presenter of *Blue Peter* was obliged to leave the programme in 1967 after his wife divorced him citing a teenage Norwegian girl he had met while filming.

25. Charles Robb. In 1991, the Democratic Senator for Virginia had an affair with Tai Collins, a former Miss Virginia, who went on to pose for *Playboy.*

26. Dwight Eisenhower. During World War Two, General Eisenhower (as he then was) had an affair with his beautiful young driver, Kay Summersby. However, according to her, it was never consummated because of the General's impotence.

27. Margaret, Duchess of Argyll. In her 1963 divorce from the Duke, photographs were produced in court of her and a mystery lover (body only). The public's curiosity in the identity of the 'headless man' helped to create the second biggest (after Profumo) scandal of the 1960s.

28. Hugh Grant. In 1995, the actor was caught in a car with hooker Divine Brown. It dented his image as a sophisticated debonair Englishman but it didn't break up his relationship with girlfriend Elizabeth Hurley.

Chapter 7

Kinky Sex

21 CELEBRITIES WHO JOINED THE MILE-HIGH CLUB

1. Bill Clinton

2. Joe McGann

3. Georgina Hale

4. Frances Ruffelle

5. Mick Hill

6. Mel B.

7. and 8. Julia Roberts and Jason Patric

9. Alan Whicker ("my safari suit got quite crumpled")

10. Tori Spelling

11. Dennis Rodman

12. Samantha Fox

13. and 14. Pamela Anderson Lee and Tommy Lee

15. and 16. John Travolta and Kelly Preston (returning from their wedding in France on a private jet back to America)

17. John Cusack

18. and 19. Daniella Westbrook and Brian Harvey

20. The Maharaja of Baroda

21. Bjorn Borg (or so he claimed. He says he did it with first wife Mariana on a flight from Copenhagen to New York, but the stewardess looking after them said it's not true and that Bjorn was reading Mickey Mouse comics)

22 CELEBRITIES WHO PARTICIPATED IN THREE-IN-A-BED 'ROMPS'

1. Jack Nicholson

2. George Gershwin

3. Jack Johnson

4. Honoré de Balzac

5. Jeff Stewart

6. Steve McFadden

7. Van Morrison (with two divorcees he met at a dinner party)

8. Samantha Janus (with a Dreamboy and his wife. She denied it but the *News of the World* had it on video)

9. Kirsten Imrie

10. Freddie Starr

11. Adam Clayton

12. Roger Moore (Ed "Kookie" Byrnes revealed in his autobiography that he and Roger mutually enjoyed a 20-year-old starlet)

13. John Leslie (took two lesbians to his hotel but apparently they only had eyes for each other)

14. Richard Spring (then a Tory MP – when it was revealed, he resigned)

15. Mick Hucknall (with two dancers)

16. Owen Oyston

17. Steve James

18. David Bowie (with Angie Bowie and others)

19. Little Richard (with Buddy Holly and a groupie)

20. Lytton Strachey (with Dora Carrington and a man)

21. Janis Joplin (with a man and a woman)

22. Britt Ekland (with Les McKeown and other women)

24 CELEBRITIES WHO PARTICIPATED IN ORGIES (i.e. four-in-a-bed or more)

1. Norman Mailer
2. Clara Bow
3. Sir Richard Burton
4. Lord Byron
5. Casanova
6. Catherine the Great
7. Cleopatra
8. Alexander Dumas Senior
9. King Farouk I
10. Errol Flynn
11. Paul Gauguin
12. Janis Joplin
13. Edmund Kean
14. John F. Kennedy
15. Guy de Maupassant
16. Elvis Presley
17. Grigori Rasputin
18. Babe Ruth
19. Marquis de Sade
20. Dudley Moore
21. Paul Gascoigne
22. Peter Stringfellow
23. John Barrymore
24. Jimi Hendrix

11 CELEBRITIES WHO HAVE/HAD A PENCHANT FOR SHOES/FEET

1. Feydor Dostoevsky (foot)

2. F. Scott Fitzgerald (foot)

3. Victor Hugo (foot)

4. Salvador Dali (foot)

5. Dick Morris (foot. For him it was a fetish which resulted in him being obliged to resign from the White House)

6. Matt Goss ("I love pedicured toes and elegant shoes")

7. Ross Kemp (toes – as revealed in the News of The World)

8. John Bryan (he sucked la Fergiana's toes)

9. Stephen Ward (the eminence grise behind the Profumo affair had a thing about black high heel shoes)

10. Charlie Sheen (foot – he's also a toe sucker)

11. Steve Coogan (according to ex-lover Katrina Russell, the comedian liked her to wear high heels in bed)

3 CELEBRITIES WHO LIKED BOTTOMS

1. Napoleon Bonaparte

2. Adolf Hitler

3. Enrico Caruso. In 1906, he was arrested for pinching a woman's bottom whilst walking around the Central Park Zoo. He was convicted and fined and it transpired that he often molested women.

21 CELEBRITIES WITH A TASTE FOR DOMINATION GAMES

1. Algernon Swinburne (liked being birched)

2. Kelsey Grammer (enjoyed being demeaned and dominated - according to "*Playboy* stunner" Tammi Alexander, in 1996)

3. Jonathan Aitken (had an affair with a Miss Whiplash in 1995 without apparently knowing that she was a pro)

4. Rudolph Valentino (liked to be dominated)

5. T.E. Lawrence (liked to be flogged)

6. Frank Bough (likes to be dominated – according to the *Sunday Mirror,* he paid £80 to "Mistress Charlotte" who worked at the 'best equipped' torture chamber in London)

7. Keith Floyd (according to a story in the *News of The World*, the TV chef likes being spanked)

8. Sylvester Stallone (had sex with a girl extra on the set of *Judge Dredd* when he was still miked up and he was heard saying "slap my butt". The next day, the crew wore t-shirts saying 'slap my butt')

9. Fyodor Dostoevsky (enjoyed corporal punishment fantasies. It is not entirely certain that he put them into practice)

10. William Gladstone (for him it was not a game. He liked to whip himself in order to punish himself for his sexual feelings and also to attempt to lessen his ardour. When he wasn't rescuing whores, of course)

11. Adolf Hitler (was a coprophiliac sadist)

12. James Joyce (loved being dominated by Nora Barnacle, his lifelong companion)

13. Jean Jacques Rousseau (a masochist who liked to be spanked)

14. Paul Verlaine (the French writer used to indulge in S & M with (female) prostitutes during his teens)

15. Arthur Rimbaud (the French poet was a confirmed sadist)

16. The Marquis de Sade (for whom sadism wasn't so much a game as a way of life. Personal motto: 'Love means always having to say you're sorry')

17. Michael Rennie (the actor used to regularly employ a whip as a sex aid)

18. Harvey Proctor (the ex-MP used to hire rent boys and spank them)

19. Ian Fleming (the author liked to whip women)

20. Lord Melbourne (the Prime Minister was known to be very keen on flagellation)

21. David Mellor (according to his ex-lover, Antonia de Sancha, ". . . he would get highly aroused when I smacked him." She also added, "He had a nice bottom and spanking was a regular part of our love-making")

13 CELEBRITIES WHO ARE/WERE VOYEURS

1. Chuck Berry (was actually sued for looking at women in the toilet of his restaurant)
2. Errol Flynn (used to watch his guests through a one-way mirror)
3. Lord Byron
4. Casanova
5. Charlie Chaplin (he had a telescope in his house that afforded him a bird's eye view of John Barrymore's bedroom)
6. King Farouk I
7. Maxim Gorki
8. Victor Hugo
9. Marquis de Sade
10. Elvis Presley
11. Henri de Toulouse-Lautrec (liked to watch lesbians)
12. Adolf Hitler
13. Dudley Moore (by the time he married Nicole Rothschild, he preferred voyeuristic sex to physical sex and so their child was conceived by artificial insemination)

4 CELEBRITIES WHO ARE EXHIBITIONISTS

1. Sylvester Stallone (filmed himself having sex with a woman by his swimming-pool)
2. Nicky Summerbee let his friends watch when he had sex with a girl
3. Errol Flynn loved to show off his manhood – especially when it was in priapic mode
4. Jean Jacques Rousseau would show off his bum in the hope that some disgusted woman would spank it.

4 CELEBRITIES AND THEIR FAVOURITE SEXUAL PREFERENCE

1. James Boswell: Trees. During his teens the great writer used to enjoy shagging trees
2. Howard Hughes: Hair. He liked his women hairy and forbade them to shave themselves
3. James Joyce: Underwear. He used to carry around a pair of doll's knickers in his pocket
4. Yukio Mishima: Sweat. He loved the smell of men's sweat. He also had a thing about white gloves

8 CELEBRITY MEN WHO LIKE/LIKED TO WEAR WOMEN'S CLOTHES

Excluding those whose work is dependent on dressing in drag i.e., Barry Humphries (aka Dame Eda Everage)

1. J. Edgar Hoover
2. Cary Grant
3. Eddie Izzard
4. Divine
5. Alexander Woollcott
6. RuPaul
7. Ed Wood Jr
8. Dan Dailey

2 CELEBRITIES WHO HAD BOTH THE MOTHER AND THE DAUGHTER (though not at the same time)

1. Les McKeown (Britt Ekland and Victoria Sellers)
2. Alan Clark (Mrs Harkness and her two daughters)

10 POPES WHO HAD SEX DURING THEIR TIME AS POPES

1. Pope Sergius III
2. Pope Balthasar Cossa
3. Pope Alexander VI
4. Pope Leo VIII
5. Pope John XII
6. Pope Benedict IX
7. Pope Paul II
8. Pope Sixtus IV
9. Pope Leo X
10. Pope Julius III

8 CELEBRITY MEN WHO CONFESSED – OFTEN IN JEST – TO BEING FRIGHTENED OF WOMEN

1. August Strindberg
2. Terry Major-Ball
3. Anthony Perkins
4. Terry Wogan
5. Harold "Dickie" Bird
6. Johann Von Goethe
7. Dudley Moore
8. Robbie Williams (or so he said in 1994, but the lad seems to have made up for it since!)

39 THINGS CELEBRITIES HAVE SAID ABOUT SEX

1. "I believe that sex is a beautiful thing between two people. Between *five,* it's fantastic . . ." (Woody Allen)

2. "When women go wrong, men go right after them" (Mae West)

3. "My father told me all about the birds and the bees. The liar – I went steady with a woodpecker till I was 21" (Bob Hope)

4. "Sex is one of the nine reasons for reincarnation – the other eight are unimportant" (Henry Miller)

5. "I know it does make people happy but to me it is just like having a cup of tea" (Cynthia Payne)

6. Sex is important, but by no means the only important thing in life" (Mary Whitehouse)

7. "Sex is about as important as a cheese sandwich. But a cheese sandwich, if you ain't got one to put in your belly, is extremely important" (Ian Dury)

8. "The only unnatural sexual behaviour is none at all" (Sigmund Freud)

9. "All this fuss about sleeping together; for physical pleasure I'd sooner go to my dentist any day" (Evelyn Waugh)

10. "I honestly prefer chocolate to sex" (Dale Winton)

11. "It's been so long since I made love, I can't remember who gets tied up" (Joan Rivers)

12. "Sex appeal is 50% what you've got and 50% what people think you've got" (Sophia Loren)

13. "I hate the whole sex scene: I'd put a bottle over the head of anybody who tried to chat me up" (Toyah Wilcox)

14. "It has to be admitted that we English have sex on the brain – which is a very unsatisfactory place to have it" (Malcolm Muggeridge)

15. "Sex – the poor man's polo" (Clifford Odets)

16. "My favourite sexual fantasy is smearing my naked body with chocolate and cream – then being left alone to lick it off" (Jo Brand)

17. "It ruins friendships between men and women" (Julia Roberts)

18. "I always thought *coq au vin* was love in a lorry" (Victoria Wood)

19. "I'm never through with a girl until I've had her three ways" (John F. Kennedy)

20. "Sex is best in the afternoon after a shower" (Ronald Reagan)

21. "The good thing about masturbation is that you don't have to dress up for it" (Truman Capote)

22. "Conventional sexual intercourse is like squirting jam into a doughnut" (Germaine Greer)

23. "The greatest pleasure that one person can offer another is carnal pleasure" (Coco Chanel)

24. "It's not terribly important in my life" (Julia McKenzie)

25. "I've never considered myself addicted to anything, but if I was, sex was it" (Clint Eastwood)

26. "What comes first in a relationship is lust, then more lust" (Jacqueline Bisset)

27. "What is a promiscuous person? It's usually someone who is getting more sex than you are" (Victor Lownes)

28. "Sex is a bad thing because it rumples the clothes" (Jacqueline Onassis)

29. "A man with an erection is in no need of advice" (Samuel Pepys)

30. "The number of available orgasms is fixed at birth and can be expended. A young man should make love very seldom or he will have nothing left for middle age" (Ernest Hemingway)

31. "Sex has never interested me much. I don't understand how people can waste so much time over sex. Sex is for kids, for movies – it's a great bore" (Sir Alfred Hitchcock)

32. "Sex is as important as food and drink" (Britt Ekland)

33. "The only unnatural sex act is that which you can not perform" (Alfred Kinsey)

34. "Some things are better than sex and some things are worse, but there's nothing exactly like it" (W C Fields)

35. "I think a man can have two, maybe three love affairs while he is married. But three is the absolute maximum. After that you are cheating" (Yves Montand)

36. "If you were married to Marilyn Monroe – you'd cheat with some ugly girl." (George Burns)

37. "The minute you start fiddling around outside the idea of monogamy, nothing satisfies anymore." (Richard Burton)

38. "Accursed from their birth they be/ Who seek to find monogamy./ Pursuing it from bed to bed /I think they would be better dead." (Dorothy Parker)

39. "You know, of course, that the Tasmanians, who never committed adultery, are now extinct." (W. Somerset Maugham)

17 UNUSUAL PLACES WHERE CELEBRITIES HAVE HAD SEX

This reminds me of a wonderful (hopefully true) story. During a roadshow of the TV game show *Mr & Mrs.* the presenter (not Derek Batey) asked a man "Where's the most unusual place you've had sex?". After some prompting, the man admitted that he and his wife had "done it" in a golf bunker on their honeymoon. His wife was then brought into the room and asked the same question. She looked to her husband for reassurance. He told her to go ahead. "Up me bum" was her reply.

1. Kate O'Mara: "On an ancient pagan site on a Sussex hillside"

2. Errol Brown: "Driving around in my car in the Bahamas. It was very difficult and very dangerous. We survived it but I wouldn't recommend it"

3. Kid Creole: "Driving in a horse-drawn buggy through Central Park"

4. Matt Aitken: "In an Inter-City loo on the way from London to Manchester"

5. Judy Cornwell: "On a diving-board"

6. Joe McGann: "In a train loo on the way from Newcastle to London"

7. Mike Stock: "In a swimming-pool"

8. Brian Glover: "In the British Museum"

9. Lennie Bennett: "On a beach in Jamaica"

10. Cathy Shipton: "In a cupboard"

11. Lynne Perrie: "On top of Table Mountain in Cape Town"

12. Ronnie Biggs: "In a train carriage"

13. Darren Day: "On the bonnet of my car in the BBC multi-storey car park"

14. Dr Fox: "While doing a radio show"

15. Sylvester Stallone: With Naomi Campbell by his swimming-pool

16. Clark Gable and Carole Lombard: In a duck blind

17. Matt Goss: Under the Eiffel Tower

1 CELEBRITY WHO EVERY TIME SHE MET A MAN SHE ADMIRED FOR THE FIRST TIME (E.G. GEORGE BERNARD SHAW) WOULD INVARIABLY UNZIP THEM AND TAKE OUT THEIR MANHOOD

1. Marlene Dietrich

6 CELEBRITIES AND THEIR FANTASIES

1. Bette Midler – being a hooker

2. Shirley Maclaine – macho men

3. Burt Reynolds – making love non-stop for 48 hours

4. John Travolta – Jane Fonda

5. Emma Bunton – Leonardo Di Caprio, or at least ". . . sitting in a pool of sweets with him"

6. Courtney Love – "I have a Michael Douglas fetish"

Chapter 8

Each to Their Own

▬▬▬▬▬▬▬▬▬▬▬▬▬▬▬

146 GAY CELEBRITIES

1. Ronnie Kray
2. Rupert Brooke
3. Allen Ginsberg
4. Andy Warhol
5. Sir Francis Bacon
6. George Michael
7. Vaslav Nijinksy
8. Molière
9. David Geffen
10. Divine
11. Graham Chapman
12. Dustin Gee
13. Tennessee Williams
14. Fred Talbot
15. Brian Epstein
16. E.M. Forster
17. Ned Sherrin
18. Harvey Fierstein
19. Dag Hammarskjold
20. Stephen Fry
21. Yukio Mishima
22. John Schlesinger
23. King James I
24. Sir Cameron Mackintosh
25. Sandro Botticelli
26. Roy Barraclough
27. Dean Sullivan
28. Socrates
29. Robert Mapplethorpe
30. Nigel Hawthorne
31. Michael Cashman
32. Boy George
33. Julian Clary
34. John Maynard Keynes
35. Charles Laughton
36. Edward Albee
37. Gore Vidal
38. Malcolm Forbes
39. James Baldwin
40. Tab Hunter
41. Quentin Crisp
42. Truman Capote
43. A.E. Housman
44. Henry James
45. Armistead Maupin
46. Christopher Marlowe
47. George Santayana
48. Ronald Allen
49. Sir John Gielgud
50. Liberace
51. Ralph Waldo Emerson
52. RuPaul
53. Marcel Proust
54. Richard Wattis
55. Yves St Laurent
56. T E Lawrence
57. Frederick the Great
58. André Gide
59. Sophocles
60. Greg Louganis
61. King Richard II
62. King Edward II
63. Franz Schubert
64. Lytton Strachey
65. Thornton Wilder
66. J. Edgar Hoover
67. Maurice Ravel
68. Alexander the Great
69. Ludwig Wittgenstein
70. Merv Griffin
71. Joe Orton
72. Kenneth Williams
73. Stephen Foster
74. Benjamin Britten
75. James Coco

76. Jean Cocteau

77. President James Buchanan

78. King William III

79. Lorenz Hart

80. Raymond Burr

81 Bill Tilden

82. Leonardo da Vinci

83. Derek Jarman

84. Clifton Webb

85. Alec McCowen

86. Sir Ian McKellen

87. Christopher Isherwood

88. Simon Fanshawe

89. W.H. Auden

90. Walt Whitman

91. Rock Hudson

92. Rudolf Nureyev

93. Alan Turing

94. Noel Coward

95. Sir Francis Bacon

96. Alexander Woollcott

97. Chris Smith

98. George Cukor

99. Gorden Kaye

100. Charles Laughton

101. Monty Woolley

102. Pier Paolo Pasolini

103. Matthew Parris

104. Russell Harty

105. Cecil Beaton

106. Cole Porter

107. Freddie Mercury

108. Peter Tchaikovsky

109. Jean Genet

110. Plato

111. Ismail Merchant

112. Peter Wyngarde

113. Michael Barrymore

114. Ian Charleson

115. Sir Terence Rattigan

116. Guy Burgess

117. King Richard I (The Lionheart)

118. Alan Bennett

119. Brendan Behan

120. Gilbert Harding

121. Sir Elton John

122. Dan Dailey

123. Christopher Biggins

124. Sir Michael Tippett

125. Sir Frederick Ashton

126. Tom Driberg

127. Jimmy Somerville

128. Leigh Bowery

129. Jeremy Thorpe

130. Lord Darnley

131. Vincente Minnelli

132. Dack Rambo

133. Kenny Everett

134. Roy Cohn

135. Serge Diaghilev

136. Arthur Rimbaud

137. Sir Arthur C. Clarke

138. Lord Alfred Douglas

139. Julius Caesar

140. Jimmy Edwards

141 Simon Raven

142. Anthony Sher

143. Simon Callow

144. William S. Burroughs

145. Rupert Everett

146. Wayne Sleep

32 LESBIAN CELEBRITIES

1. Martina Navratilova
2. George Sand
3. Miriam Margolyes
4. Dame Ivy Compton-Burnett
5. Gertrude Stein
6. Queen Christina of Sweden
7. Pat Arrowsmith
8. Alice B. Toklas
9. Pam St Clement
10. Billie-Jean King
11. Sophie Ward
12. Linda Bellos
13. Virginia Woolf
14. Vita Sackville-West
15. Sandi Toksvig
16. Katherine Mansfield
17. Maureen Colquhoun
18. Radclyffe Hall
19. Bessie Smith
20. Edith Wharton
21. Edith Head
22. Agnes Moorehead
23. Sandy Dennis
24. Capucine
25. Nancy Kulp
26. Joan of Arc (or so it is now believed)
27. Rachel Williams
28. Sandra Bernhard
29. Hufty
30. Kate Millett
31. Angela Eagle MP
32. Ellen DeGeneres

84 BISEXUAL CELEBRITIES

(Note: many of these people will have gone/are going for long periods at a time where they are either exclusively straight or exclusively gay. In the case of living people, they might now be exclusively straight.

However, they are on this list because for some length of time in their lives, they have had relationships with both genders – although not necessarily concurrently.)

1. Frankie Howerd
2. Josephine Baker
3. Marlene Dietrich
4. Greta Garbo
5. Nero
6. Caligula
7. Pompey
8. Alexander the Great
9. Aristotle
10. Barbara Stanwyck
11. Ludwig van Beethoven
12. Sandro Botticelli
13. Lord Byron
14. Anaîs Nin
15. W. Somerset Maugham
16. Michelangelo
17. John Milton
18. Plato
19. Marcel Proust
20. William Shakespeare
21. Socrates

22. Tyrone Power

23. Errol Flynn

24. Peter The Great

25. Maurice Chevalier

26. Marie Antoinette

27. Maria Schneider

28. Colette

29. Isadora Duncan

30. Mata Hari

31. Queen Anne

32. Eleanor Roosevelt

33. Lady Emma Hamilton

34. Catherine the Great

35. Tallulah Bankhead

36. James Dean

37. Denholm Elliott

38. Tony Richardson

39. Sir Michael Redgrave

40. Rachel Williams

41. Edwina Mountbatten

42. Leonard Bernstein

43. Montgomery Clift

44. Helmut Berger

45. Sir Richard Burton

46. George Eliot

47. Algernon Swinburne

48. Paul Verlaine

49. George Melly

50. Tom Robinson

51. Janis Joplin

52. Bessie Smith

53. Julie Goodyear

54. Judy Holliday

55. Jacqueline Susann

56. Ethel Merman

57. Angie Bowie

58. David Bowie

59. Alan Freeman

60. Aleister Crowley

61. Joe Longthorne

62. Calvin Klein

63. Jann Wenner

64. Anna Nicole Smith

65. Richard Fairbrass

66. Buddy Holly (according to Little Richard)

67. Barry Evans

68. Beatrice Lillie

69. Dennis Rodman

70. Robert Downey Junior

71. Whitney Houston

72. Michael Stipe

73. Kit Hesketh-Harvey

74. Siegfried Sassoon

75. Anthony Perkins

76. Randolph Scott

77. Howard Hughes

78. Cary Grant

79. Bruce Chatwin

80. Bob Boothby

81. Laurence Harvey

82. Salvador Dali

26 PREDOMINANTLY STRAIGHT CELEBRITIES WHO HAD ONE (OR MORE) GAY EXPERIENCE

1. Hugh Hefner
2. Marlon Brando
3. Pete Townshend
4. John Lennon (apparently with Brian Epstein)
5. Rod McKuen
6. Casanova
7. Marcello Mastroianni
8. Daryl Hall
9. Richard Burton
10. Gary Cooper
11. Tiny Tim
12. Voltaire
13. Robert Graves (in his youth)
14. Oliver Stone
15. David Niven
16. Harold Robbins
17. Leo Tolstoy
18. Alan Paton
19. Carl Jung
20. Lord Laurence Olivier
21. D.H. Lawrence
22. King Charles II
23. John Osborne
24. Sir Winston Churchill
25. Mick Jagger
26. Sir John Betjeman

23 PREDOMINANTLY STRAIGHT CELEBRITIES WHO HAD ONE (OR MORE) LESBIAN EXPERIENCE

1. Marianne Faithfull
2. Janis Joplin
3. Madonna
4. Billie Holiday (the first time she was in prison)
5. Joan Crawford
6. Edith Piaf
7. Cher (she admitted to having relationships with women in the course of an interview with her daughter Chastity, for *The Advocate,* a gay magazine)
8. Grace Jones
9. Joan Baez
10. Judy Carne
11. Marilyn Monroe
12. Coco Chanel
13. Emma Thompson (according to the front page of *The News of The World* in April 1998)
14. Judy Holliday
15. Miriam Hopkins
16. Janet Gaynor
17. Mary Martin
18. Judy Garland
19. Myrna Loy
20. Sharon Stone
21. Louise Brooks
22. Hattie McDaniel
23. Dame Sybil Thorndyke

29 GAY AND BISEXUAL CELEBRITIES WHO MARRIED WOMEN

1. Andre Gide
2. Oscar Wilde
3. Lord Alfred Douglas
4. Julius Caesar
5. Peter Tchaikovsky
6. W.H. Auden (married Erika Mann to save her from the Nazis)
7. King Edward II
8. Sir Elton John
9. Rock Hudson
10. Kenny Everett
11. Raymond Burr
12. Ronald Allen
13. Vaslav Nijinsky
14. Jimmy Edwards
15. King James I
16. Cole Porter
17. Alexander the Great
18. Yukio Mishima
19. Simon Raven
20. Charles Laughton
21. Michael Barrymore
22. Ronnie Kray
23. Malcolm Forbes
24. Dan Dailey
25. Vincente Minnelli
26. Christopher Biggins
27. Jeremy Thorpe (twice)
28. Tom Driberg
29. Sir Arthur C. Clarke

8 CELEBRITIES WHO MARRIED GAY MEN

1. Elsa Lanchester (Charles Laughton)
2. Vanessa Redgrave (Tony Richardson)
3. Angela Lansbury (Richard Cromwell)
4. Su Pollard (Peter Keogh)
5. Mary, Queen of Scots (Lord Darnley)
6. Sue Lloyd (Ronald Allen)
7. Judy Garland (Vincente Minnelli)
8. Liza Minnelli (Peter Allen. Interestingly, Judy and Liza both had gay fathers and both married gay men. No wonder gays call themselves 'friends of Dorothy' after Judy's character in The Wizard of Oz)

17 GAY RELATIONSHIPS BETWEEN CELEBRITIES

1. Tyrone Power and Lorenz Hart
2. Cole Porter and 'Black' Jack Bouvier (Jackie O's father)
3. Errol Flynn and Tyrone Power
4. Errol Flynn and Truman Capote
5. Howard Hughes and Tyrone Power
6. Allen Ginsberg and Jack Kerouac (or so Ginsberg claimed)
7. Gary Cooper and Cecil Beaton
8. Stephen Spender (a straight virgin at the time) and W.H. Auden
9. Lord Laurence Olivier and Danny Kaye (or so some biographers have claimed)
10. Vaslav Nijinsky and Serge Diaghilev
11. Christopher Isherwood and W.H. Auden
12. Arthur Rimbaud and Paul Verlaine
13. Peter Hudson and David Halls
14. Howard Hughes and Cary Grant
15. Cary Grant and Randolph Scott
16. Howard Hughes and Randolph Scott
17. Sir Winston Churchill and Ivor Novello

Note: Jim Morrison and Jimi Hendrix. (Morrison once undid Hendrix's trousers while Hendrix was performing and fellated him)

15 LESBIAN RELATIONSHIPS BETWEEN CELEBRITIES

1. Dolores Del Rio & Greta Garbo
2. Barbara Stanwyck & Joan Crawford
3. Greta Garbo & Louise Brooks
4. Jacqueline Susann & Ethel Merman
5. Janet Gaynor & Mary Martin
6. Hattie McDaniel & Tallulah Bankhead
7. Josephine Baker & Colette
8. Tallulah Bankhead & Billie Holiday
9. Tallulah Bankhead & Beatrice Lillie
10. Tallulah Bankhead & Dame Sybil Thorndyke
11. Joan Crawford & Martha Raye
12. Marlene Dietrich & Edith Piaf
13. Barbara Stanwyck & Marlene Dietrich
14. Greta Garbo & Beatrice Lillie
15. Judy Garland & Ethel Merman

8 LESBIAN AND BISEXUAL CELEBRITIES WHO MARRIED MEN

1. Katherine Mansfield
2. Billie-Jean King
3. Virginia Woolf
4. Vita Sackville-West
5. Bessie Smith
6. Pam St Clement
7. Capucine
8. Sophie Ward

4 CELEBRITY MEN WHO MARRIED LESBIANS

1. August Strindberg
2. Havelock Ellis
3. Harold Nicolson
4. Rudolph Valentino (twice)

5 CELEBRITIES WITH HOMOSEXUAL PARENTS

1. Patrick Macnee (mother)
2. Nigel Nicolson (mother)
3. Judy Garland (father)
4. Jacqueline Onassis (father)
5. Liza Minnelli (father)

7 CELEBRITIES WITH HOMOSEXUAL CHILDREN

1. Cher
2. Barbra Streisand & 3. Elliot Gould
4. Simon Ward
5. Sir Anthony Eden
6. Stanley Baldwin
7. Lynn Redgrave

26 CELEBRITIES WHO PAID FOR SEX WITH MALE PROSTITUTES

1. Sir Arthur C. Clarke

2. George Cukor

3. Howard Hughes

4. Roy Cohn

5. A.E. Housman

6. Gorden Kaye ('. . . on three or four occasions . . . which I realize now was very silly. But I have never done anything illegal. And I have certainly never knowingly been with anyone underage')

7. Charles Laughton

8. Joe Orton

9. Leonardo da Vinci

10. Monty Woolley

11. Cole Porter

12. Pier Paolo Pasolini

13. Harvey Proctor

14. T.E. Lawrence

15. Russell Harty

16. Cecil Beaton

17. Errol Flynn

18. W. Somerset Maugham

19. Montgomery Clift

20. André Gide

21. Christopher Isherwood

22. Yukio Mishima

23. Oscar Wilde

24. Lord Alfred Douglas

25. J. Edgar Hoover

26. Brian Epstein

4 CELEBRITIES WHO ADMITTED TO WORKING AS MALE PROSTITUTES AT LEAST ONCE

1. Rupert Everett

2. Jean Genet

3. Octavius

4. Robert Mapplethorpe

9 CELEBRITIES WHO HAVE BEEN PROSECUTED FOR GAY 'CRIMES'

1. Sir John Gielgud. In 1953, the great actor was fined £15 after pleading guilty to a charge of 'importuning' in a public lavatory. In an attempt to avoid publicity, Gielgud listed his occupation as 'clerk'.

2. Peter Wyngarde. In 1975, the actor best known as Jason King in *Department S* was arrested in a public toilet and accused of committing an act of gross indecency with a Gloucester crane driver. He was fined £75 but, worse still, his career nose-dived.

3. Leonardo da Vinci. At the age of 24, he was arrested for going with a 17-year-old male prostitute and was jailed for a short time before his friends could release him.

4. Montgomery Clift. Just after becoming famous, the actor was arrested for trying to pick up a male prostitute in New York.

5. Oscar Wilde. Wilde started a libel case against the father of his lover, Lord Alfred Douglas, for calling him a sodomite, which he lost. This led to a criminal trial in which he was sentenced to two years hard labour in Reading Gaol, where he wrote his immortal Ballad.

6. Alan Turing. The mathematical genius who broke the German Enigma code (and thus helped us to win World War Two) was charged with "gross indecency" for his relationship with a 19-year-old boy. He was put on probation and given 'treatment' for his homosexuality which may have been a possible cause of his suicide two years later. His story was brilliantly adapted for the stage by Hugh Whitemore in the play *Breaking The Code* with Sir Derek Jacobi playing Turing.

7. Bill Tilden. The great American tennis player was arrested in 1964 and sent to a California "honor farm" for 'contributing to the delinquency of a minor'. This basically ruined him.

8. George Michael. In 1998, the singer was arrested for 'lewd behaviour' (i.e. cottaging) in a Californian park toilet.

9. Tom Driberg. The former Labour MP and journalist was caught cottaging on more than one occasion but his boss, Lord Beaverbrook, managed to get the charges dropped.

THE AGE AT WHICH 10 GAY CELEBRITIES HAD THEIR FIRST GAY SEX

1. Boy George (15 – with a man of 45)

2. Noel Coward (17)

3. Tennessee Williams (28)

4. E.M. Forster (31)

5. W. Somerset Maugham (16)

6. Oscar Wilde (32 – with Robbie Ross)

7. André Gide (23 – with a 14-year old Tunisian boy)

8. Christopher Biggins (25)

9. Julian Clary (19)

10. Harvey Fierstein (13)

12 STRAIGHT CELEBRITIES WHO ARE GAY ICONS

1. Shirley Bassey

2. Judy Garland

3. Liza Minnelli

4. The Beverley Sisters

5. Marilyn Monroe

6. Bette Midler

7. Dolly Parton

8. Elizabeth Taylor

9. Barbara Windsor

10. Kylie Minogue

11. Diana Ross

12. Barbra Streisand

Chapter 9

Love for Sale

47 ACTORS WHO SHED THEIR CLOTHES IN FILMS

1. Robert De Niro in *1900* (1976).

2. John Malkovich, in *The Sheltering Sky* (1990).

3. Tom Cruise, in *All The Right Moves* (1983).

4. Robin Williams in *The Fisher King* (1991)

5. Pierce Brosnan, in *Live Wire* (1992).

6. Sean Bean, in *Stormy Weather* (1988).

7. Harvey Keitel in *The Piano* (1993).

8. Kevin Bacon in *Pyratea* (1991).

9. Patrick Swayze in *Roadhouse* (1989).

10. Michael Douglas in *Basic Instinct* (1992).

11. Robert Carlyle in *The Full Monty* (1997)

12. Tom Berenger in *At Play in the Fields of the Lord* (1991)

13. Dennis Hopper in *Nails* (1992)

14. Mel Gibson in *Lethal Weapon* (1987).

15. David Hasselhoff in *Return of the Cheerleaders* (1976).

16. John Cleese in *Romance with a Double Bass* (1974).

17. Sean Connery in *The Man Who Would be King* (1975).

18. Rob Lowe in *Bad Influence* (1990).

19. Nick Nolte in *Weeds* (1987).

20. Nicholas Cage in *Zandalee* (1991).

21. Albert Finney in *Under the Volcano* (1984).

22. Alec Baldwin in *The Getaway* (1993).

23. Johnny Depp in *Private Resort* (1985).

24. Peter Fonda in *Molly and Gina* (1993).

25. Michael J Fox in *Greedy* (1993).

26. Richard Gere in *Final Analysis* (1992).

27. Gerard Depardieu in *1900* (1976).

28. Arnold Schwarzenegger in *The Terminator* (1984).

29. Jean-Claude Van Damme in *Universal Soldier* (1992).

30. Denzel Washington in *Mississippi Masala* (1992).

31. Mathew Broderick in *Out on a Limb* (1992).

32. Jeremy Irons in *Damage* (1992).

33. Jeff Bridges in *Winter Kills* (1979).

34. Kevin Kline in *Consenting Adults* (1992).

35. Michael York in *Justine* (1969).

36. Malcolm McDowell in *If . . .* (1969).

37. Stacy Keach in *The Squeeze* (1977).

38. William Dafoe *in Body of Evidence* (1992).

39. Dennis Quaid in *The Big Easy* (1987).

40. Richard Harris in *A Man Called Horse* (1970).

41. Eric Stoltz in *Haunted Summer* (1988).

42. John Hurt in *East of Elephant Rock* (1976).

43. Sir Ian McKellen in *Priest of Love* (1980)

44. Kevin Costner in *Dances with Wolves* (1990).

45. & 46. Alan Bates and Oliver Reed in *Women in Love* (1971).

47. Ewan McGregor in *The Pillow Book* (1996).

67 ACTRESSES WHO SHED THEIR CLOTHES IN FILMS

1. Susan Sarandon, in *Pretty Baby* (1978).

2. Jodie Foster, in *Backtrack* (1981).

3. Helena Bonham Carter, in *The Wings of A Dove* (1998).

4. Laura Dern, in *Wild At Heart* (1990).

5. Melanie Griffith, in *Something Wild* (1986).

6. Nicole Kidman, in *Windrider* (1986)

7. Daryl Hannah, in *Reckless* (1984)

8. Rosanna Arquette, in *The Executioner's Song* (1982).

9. Glenn Close, in *Fatal Attraction* (1987).

10. Bridget Fonda, in *Aria* (1987).

11. Ursula Andress, in *Loaded Guns* (1975).

12. Natasha Richardson, in *A Handmaid's Tale* (1990).

13. Phoebe Cates, in *Fast Times at Ridgemont High* (1982).

14. Ellen Burstyn, in *Tropic of Cancer* (1970).

15. Stephanie Beacham, in *The Nightcomers* (1971).

16. Kate Winslet, in *Titanic* (1997).

17. Juliette Binoche, in the French film, *Rendez-vous* (1986).

18. Genevieve Bujold, in *Monsignor* (1982).

19. Kim Basinger, in *Nine and a Half Weeks* (1986).

20. Pauline Collins, in *Shirley Valentine* (1989).

21. Jenny Seagrove, in *The Guardian* (1990)

22. Valerie Kaprisky, in *Breathless* (1983)

23. Jamie Lee Curtis, in *Trading Places* (1983).

24. Julie Andrews, in *Duet for One* (1987)

25. Beverly D'Angelo, in *Hair* (1979)

26. Demi Moore, in *Striptease* (1996).

27. Uma Thurman, in *Dangerous Liaisons* (1988).

28. Susan Dey, in *First Love* (1977).

29. Angie Dickinson, in *Big Bad Mamma* (1974)

30. Holly Hunter in, *The Piano* (1993).

31. Britt Ekland in, *The Wicker Man* (1973).

32. Mia Farrow in, *A Wedding* (1978).

33. Sherilyn Fenn, in *Boxing Helena* (1993).

34. Susan George in, *Straw Dogs* (1972).

35. Samantha Janus, in *Up 'n' Under* (1998).

36. Teri Hatcher, in *The Cool Surface* (1992).

37. Maria Hemingway, in *Star 80* (1983)

38. Sissy Spacek, in *Prime Cut* (1972).

39. Helen Hun, in *The Waterdance* (1991).

40. Sigourney Weaver, in *Half Moon Street* (1986).

41. Isabelle Hupert, in *Heaven's Gate* (1980).

42. Glenda Jackson, in *Women in Love* (1971).

43. Barbara Carrera, in *Point of Impact* (1983).

44. Catherine Deneuve, in *Lovers Like Us* (1975).

45. Patsy Kensit, in *Bitter Harvest* (1993).

46. Deborah Kerr, in *The Gypsy Moths* (1969).

47. Nastassja Kinski, in *Cat People* (1982).

48. Debra Winger, in *An Officer and a Gentleman* (1982).

49. Phyllis Logan, in *Another Time, Another Place* (1983).

50. Shirley Maclaine, in *Desperate Characters* (1971)

51. Diane Keaton, in *Looking for Mr. Goodbar* (1977)

52. Helen Mirren, in *Savage Messiah* (1972).

53. Joely Richardson, in *Drowning by Numbers* (1988).

54. Miranda Richardson, in *Damage* (1992).

55. Rebecca De Mornay, in *And God Created Woman* (1988).

56. Greta Scacchi, in *A Man in Love* (1987).

57. Ann-Margret, in *Magic* (1978)

58. Maryam D'Abo, in *Xtro* (1982).

59. Sharon Stone, in *Basic Instinct* (1992).

60. Emma Thompson, in *The Tall Guy* (1990).

61. Hayley Mills, in *Deadly Strangers* (1974).

62. Kathleen Turner, in *Crimes of Passion* (1984)

63. Amanda Donohue, in *Castaway* (1986)

64. Jennifer Jason Leigh, in *Single White Female* (1992)

65. Annette Benning, in *The Grifters* (1990).

66. Robin Givens, in *A Rage In Harlem* (1991).

67. Ellen Barkin, in *Siesta* (1987).

3 PORN STARS WHO BECAME FULLY CLOTHED CELEBRITIES

1. Linda Lovelace
2. Marilyn Chambers
3. Bambi Woods

5 PIN-UP GIRLS WHO BECAME FULLY CLOTHED CELEBRITIES

1. Samantha Fox
2. Linda Lusardi
3. Jilly Johnson
4. Melinda Messenger
5. Kathy Lloyd

28 CELEBRITIES WHO WERE BEAUTY QUEENS

1. Shakira Caine (Miss Guyana)
2. Marla Maples (Miss Georgia Peach)
3. Leila Williams (Miss Great Britain)
4. Vicki Oyston (Miss Fleetwood)
5. Veronica Lake (Miss Florida)
6. Desiree Washington (Miss Rhode Island)
7. Kim Novak (Miss Deepfreeze)
8. Carolyn Seaward (Miss UK)
9. Anita Ekberg (Miss Sweden)
10. Pamella Bordes (Miss India)
11. Imelda Marcos (Miss Manila)
12. Jayne Mansfield (Miss Flash)
13. Lynda Carter (Miss America)
14. Meg Gallagher (Miss Holiday Guernsey)
15. Dorothy Lamour (Miss New Orleans)
16. Carol Smillie (Miss Parallel Bars)
17. Sylvie Kristel (Miss TV Europe)
18. Gina Lollobrigida (Miss Italy)
19. Debbie Greenwood (Miss Great Britain)
20. Sophia Loren (Miss Elegance)
21. Michelle Pfeiffer (Miss Orange County)
22. Raquel Welch (Miss Photogenic)
23. Debbie Reynolds (Miss Burbank)
24. Lauren Bacall (Miss Greenwich Village)
25. Zsa Zsa Gabor (Miss Hungary)
26. Dyan Cannon (Miss West Seattle)
27. Cybill Shepherd (Miss Teenage Memphis)
28. Kim Basinger (Miss Junior Athens)

10 NOTABLY NAMED AMERICAN PORN STARS

1. Blonde Ice
2. Ebony Ayes
3. Purple Passion
4. Long Dan Silver
5. September Raines
6. Kayla Kleavage
7. Lisa Lipps
8. Wendy Whoppers
9. Brandi Wine
10. Sharon Swallow

6 CELEBRITIES WHO HAVE APPEARED IN (VERY) SOFT PORN FILMS

1. David Duchovny in *New Year's Day* (1989)
2. Joan Crawford in *The Casting Couch* (no date available but it was in the days before she became Joan Crawford)
3. Joanna Lumley in *Games Lovers Play* (1970)
4. Sylvester Stallone in *A Party at Kitty and Stud's* (1970)
5. Lynda Bellingham in *Confessions of a Driving Instructorr* (1976)
6. Diane Keen in *Sex Thief* (1973)

4 CELEBRITIES WHO WERE PLAYBOY BUNNIES

1. Debbie Harry
2. Gloria Steinem (on an undercover assignment)
3. Lauren Hutton
4. Fiona Richmond

28 CELEBRITIES WHO STRIPPED OFF FOR *PLAYBOY*

1. Kim Basinger
2. Amanda de Cadenet
3. Joan Collins
4. Lysette Anthony
5. Victoria Sellers
6. Farrah Fawcett
7. Patti Reagan
8. Dannii Minogue
9. Margot Hemingway
10. Cindy Crawford
11. Samantha Fox
12. Marilyn Monroe
13. Sharon Stone
14. Rachel Williams
15. Drew Barrymore
16. Bo Derek
17. Catherine Deneuve
18. Sherilyn Fenn
19. Carla Bruni
20. Mimi Rogers
21. Alessandra Mussolini
22. Shannen Doherty
23. Pamela Anderson
24. Robin Givens
25. Sandra Bernhard
26. Elle Macpherson
27. Anna Nicole Smith
28. Jayne Mansfield

10 CELEBRITIES WHO *REFUSED* TO STRIP OFF FOR *PLAYBOY*

1. Teri Hatcher
2. Melissa Bell
3. Heather Locklear
4. Steffi Graf
5. Yasmine Bleeth
6. Marla Trump
7. Patsy Kensit
8. Raquel Welch
9. Priscilla Presley
10. Debbie Gibson

7 CELEBRITIES WHO HAVE STRIPPED OFF FOR WOMEN'S MAGAZINES

1. Burt Reynolds
2. Fabian
3. Paul de Feu
4. Antoine de Caunes
5. Kyran Bracken
6. David Chokachi
7. Robin Askwith

8 PEOPLE WHO BECAME CELEBRITIES BY WRITING ABOUT SEX

1. Alfred Kinsey

2. Alex Comfort

3. Shere Hite

4. Martin Cole

5. William Masters and

6. Virginia Johnson

7. Havelock Ellis

8. Vatsyayana

21 CELEBRITIES WHO LOST THEIR VIRGINITY WITH PROSTITUTES

1. Henry Fonda

2. David Niven (with a London girl nicknamed Nessie)

3. Clifford Irving

4. Uri Geller (with a Greek-Cypriot girl named Lola)

5. Charlie Sheen

6. Anton Chekhov

7. Chris De Burgh (with a French girl)

8. Simon Raven

9. Tony Mortimer

10. The Duke of Windsor

11. Napoleon Bonaparte

12. James Boswell

13. James Bond (with a prostitute named Martha Debrant in Paris, aged 16)

14. James Joyce

15. John F. Kennedy (the girl charged $3)

16. Benito Mussolini

17. Stendhal

18. Leo Tolstoy

19. H.G. Wells

20. Groucho Marx

21. Mike Tyson

78 CELEBRITIES WHO HAD SEX WITH PROSTITUTES

1. Elvis Presley
2. David Niven
3. John F. Kennedy
4. Charlie Chaplin
5. Duke Ellington
6. Henry Fonda
7. Vincent Van Gogh
8. Clark Gable
9. Jean-Paul Sartre
10. Errol Flynn
11. George Gissing
12. Victor Hugo
13. Duke of York (the eighteenth century one *not* the twentieth century one!)
14. Judah (as in The Bible)
15. John Keats
16. Henri de Toulouse-Lautrec
17. Oscar Wilde (contracted syphilis from one when at university)
18. Frank Bough
19. Benny Hill (according to Barry Took, who wrote a biography of him)
20. Georges Simenon
21. Adam Clayton
22. Robert De Niro (although he claims that he didn't pay!)
23. Casanova
24. Honoré de Balzac
25. John Barrymore
26. Napoleon Bonaparte
27. James Boswell
28. Johannes Brahms
29. Sir Richard Burton
30. Lord Byron
31. King Charles II
32. Fyodor Dostoevsky
33. Alexander Dumas Senior
34. King Edward VII
35. Guy de Maupassant
36. F. Scott Fitzgerald
37. Paul Gauguin
38. George Gershwin
39. Francisco de Goya
40. Ernest Hemingway
41. James Joyce
42. Jack London
43. W. Somerset Maugham
44. Amedeo Modigliani
45. Benito Mussolini
46. Napoleon III
47. Friedrich Nietzsche

48. Vaslav Nijinsky

49. Grigori Rasputin

50. Jean Jacques Rousseau

51. Peter Paul Rubens

52. Marquis de Sade

53. Stendhal

54. Algernon Swinburne

55. Leo Tolstoy

56. Paul Verlaine

57. H.G. Wells

58. Dudley Moore

59. Diego Maradona (who ordered 20 prostitutes to be sent up to his room at the Dorchester and then had sex with one of them)

60. Johnny Bryan

61. Al Capone

62. Andre Gide

63. Maxim Gorki (lived with a prostitute to 'reform' her)

64. 'Gentleman' Jim Corbett

65. Edmund Kean

66. Herman 'Babe' Ruth

67. Groucho Marx

68. Clifford Irving

69. Uri Geller

70. Charlie Sheen

71. Anton Chekhov

72. Chris De Burgh

73. Simon Raven

74. Tony Mortimer

75. The Duke of Windsor

76. Grover Cleveland

77. The Duke of Wellington (the Iron Duke _– not the present one!)

78. Mike Tyson

Note: Hans Christian Andersen used to go to brothels to talk with the girls

3 MEN WHO MARRIED PROSTITUTES

1. John Wayne

2. President Sidano

3. Juan Peron

15 CELEBRITIES WHO HAVE WORKED AS PROSTITUTES

1. Christine Keeler

2. Mandy Rice-Davies

3. Nell Gwyn

4. Fiona Wright

5. Pamella Bordes

6. Billie Holiday

7. Victoria Sellers

8. Kitty Fisher

9. Mata Hari

10. Eva Peron

11. Janis Joplin (in her teens, she tried – without much success – to sell herself for $5 a time.

12. Marilyn Monroe. As a struggling actress in Hollywood, Marilyn would provide 'in-car sex' in exchange for restaurant meals.

13. Carole Landis

14. Jeanette MacDonald worked as an 'escort' in New York before becoming famous

15. Lupe Velez

1 CELEBRITY WHO TURNED DOWN MONEY FOR SEX

1. Joan Collins. Her first husband, Maxwell Reed, lined up a rich Arab in return for a lot of money, but Joan gave him the about-turn *and* dumped Reed for good measure.

4 CELEBRITIES WHOSE MOTHERS WERE PROSTITUTES OR COURTESANS

1. Sarah Bernhardt
2. Clara Bow
3. Lupe Velez
4. Mary Bell

6 CELEBRITIES WHO SPENT TIME IN BROTHELS AS CHILDREN

1. James Brown
2. Louis Armstrong
3. Chico Marx (he played the piano in one)
4. Harpo Marx (he also played the piano but only knew two songs, which he played over and over again at different speeds)
5. Edith Piaf (her grandmother was the cook. She also lived in one as an adult during the German occupation because it was one of the few buildings in Paris that was heated)
6. Richard Pryor (his grandmother was the owner)

Note: Henri de Toulouse-Lautrec lived in a brothel as an adult

Chapter 10

Sex Polls

100 CELEBRITIES WHO MADE THE LIST OF *COSMOPOLITAN'S* 100 SEXIEST MEN ALIVE IN 1997. (Listed in no particular order)

1. Ray Fearon
2. Ben Chaplin
3. Tam Williams
4. Edward Atterton
5. Ronan Keating
6. William Trevitt
7. Adam Cooper
8. Tim Vincent
9. Gary Barlow
10. Simon Gregson
11. Toby Stephens
12. Jared Leto
13. Dominic West
14. Alec Baldwin
15. Stephen Baldwin
16. William Baldwin
17. Ralph Fiennes
18. Joe Fiennes
19. Noel Gallagher
20. Liam Gallagher
21. Colin Firth
22. Jonathan Firth
23. Woody Harrelson
24. Mark Lamarr
25. David Duchovny
26. John Goodman
27. Denis Leary
28. Will Smith
29. Stephen Jones
30. Robbie Coltrane
31. Ethan Hawke
32. Harry Enfield
33. Jeremy Paxman
34. Tim Jeffries
35. Eddie Irvine
36. Stephen Dorff
37. Sting
38. Jean-Marc Barr
39. Rufus Sewell
40. Johnny Depp
41. Jason Patric
42. Ray Liotta

43. Greg Wise

44. Sean Bean

45. David Schwimmer

46. Andy Garcia

47. Antonio Banderas

48. Antonio Sabato Junior

49. Joaquin Cortes

50. Patrik Berger

51. Tarquin Southwell

52. Peter Phillips

53. Trojan (Mark Griffin)

54. Martin Offiah

55. Mark Ramprakash

56. Jamie Redknapp

57. Ryan Giggs

58. Les Ferdinand

59. David Chockachi

60. Matthew McConaughey

61. Matthew Perry

62. Matt Dillon

63. Christian Slater

64. Dean Cain

65. Chris O'Donnell

66. Noah Wyle

67. Jon Bon Jovi

68. Kyle Maclachlan

69. Johnathan Schaech

70. Paul Weller

71. Crispin Mills

72. Paul Nicholls

73. Mark Owen

74. Damon Albarn

75. Brett Anderson

76. Alan Rickman

77. Tony Blair

78. Robert De Niro

79. John Malkovich

80. Jack Nicholson

81. Gerard Depardieu

82. John Travolta

83. Val Kilmer

84. Richard Gere

85. Denzel Washington

86. Mel Gibson

87. Aidan Quinn

88. Liam Neeson

89. Tom Cruise

90. Pierce Brosnan

91. George Clooney

92. Matt Le Blanc

93. Daniel Day-Lewis

94. Jeff Goldblum

95. Jarvis Cocker

96. Gabriel Byrne

97. Keanu Reeves

98. Ewan McGregor

99. Brad Pitt

100. David Ginola

100 CELEBRITIES WHOSE NAMES APPEARED IN FHM's LIST OF THE SEXIEST WOMEN IN THE WORLD IN 1998

1. Jenny McCarthy
2. Denise Van Outen
3. Louise Nurding
4. Jennifer Aniston
5. Cameron Diaz
6. Carmen Electra
7. Catherine Deeley
8. Melanie Sykes
9. Courtney Cox
10. Gillian Anderson
11. Isla Fisher
12. Yasmine Bleeth
13. Dannii Minogue
14. Natalie Imbruglia
15. Teri Hatcher
16. Alicia Silverstone
17. Kate Winslet
18. Caprice Bourret
19. Sophie Anderton
20. Melanie Blatt
21. Samantha Janus
22. Kylie Minogue
23. Sandra Bullock
24. Elizabeth Hurley
25. Melinda Messenger
26. Rhona Mitra
27. Emma Noble
28. Nicole Appleton
29. Kelly Brook
30. Tiffani Amber-Thiesson
31. Neve Campbell
32. Natalie Appleton
33. Joanne Guest
34. Salma Hayek
35. Victoria Adams
36. Cindy Crawford
37. Nicola Charles
38. Anna Friel
39. Pamela Anderson
40. Zoë Ball
41. Dani Behr
42. Tyra Banks
43. Shania Twain
44. Emma Bunton
45. Jordan
46. Mariah Carey
47. Helena Christensen
48. Kate Moss
49. Drew Barrymore
50. Ulrika Jonsson
51. Martine McCutcheon
52. Demi Moore
53. Lisa Kudrow
54. Angelica Bridges
55. Melissa George
56. Kemberley Davies

57. Winona Ryder
58. Geri Halliwell
59. Tina Hobley
60. Elle Macpherson
61. Davina McCall
62. Uma Thurman
63. Kathy Lloyd
64. Philippa Forrester
65. Traci Bingham
66. Gwyneth Paltrow
67. Natasha Henstridge
68. Liv Tyler
69. Claire Danes
70. Elisabeth Shue
71. Emmanuelle Beart
72. Catalina
73. Meg Ryan
74. Anna Kournikova
75. Claudia Schiffer
76. Donna D'Errico
77. Jayne Middlemiss
78. Mel Chisholm

79. Kirsty Wright
80. Vendela
81. Sarah Michelle Gellar
82. Sharon Stone
83. Yasmin le Bon
84. Catherine Zeta Jones
85. Emma Harrison
86. Davina Taylor
87. Eva Herzigova
88. Sara Cox
89. Lucy Lawless
90. Melanie Brown
91. Jennifer Love Hewitt
92. Tea Leoni
93. Halle Berry
94. Claire Goose
95. Natalia Cigliuti
96. Nicole Kidman`
97. Gena Lee Nolin
98. Melissa Tkautz
99. Helen Baxendale
100. Renee Zellweger

THE 10 MALE POLITICIANS WOMEN FOUND MOST ATTRACTIVE (according to a 1996 NOP poll)

1. Peter Mandelson
2. Paddy Ashdown
3. Tony Blair
4. Michael Portillo
5. Stephen Dorrell
6. Gordon Brown
7. John Redwood
8. Michael Heseltine
9. John Major
10. Ken Livingstone

THE 10 MALE POLITICIANS WOMEN FOUND LEAST ATTRACTIVE (according to a 1996 NOP poll)

1. David Mellor
2. John Prescott
3. John Major
4. Ken Livingstone
5. Michael Heseltine
6. Dennis Skinner
7. David Blunkett
8. Kenneth Clarke
9. Michael Howard
10. Jack Straw

50 CELEBRITIES WHO MADE *PEOPLE* MAGAZINE'S 1997 LIST OF THE 50 MOST BEAUTIFUL PEOPLE IN THE WORLD (in no particular order)

1. Gillian Anderson
2. Lauren Bacall
3. Jacinda Barrett
4. Drew Barrymore
5. David Baldacci
6. Toni Braxton
7. Juliette Binoche
8. Andre Braugher
9. Jim Carrey
10. Deana Carter
11. David Chokachi
12. Tom Cruise
13. Christopher Cuomo
14. Claire Danes
15. Oscar De La Hoya
16. Kamar do los Reyes
17. Leonardo DiCaprio
18. Roma Downey
19. Michael Flatley
20. Harrison Ford
21. Tom Ford
22. Vivica A. Fox
23. Cuba Gooding Junior
24. Jeff Gordon
25. Mia Hamm
26. Derek Jeter
27. Lisa Kudrow
28. Matt Lauer
29. Lucy Lawless
30. Jared Leto
31. Jennifer Lopez
32. Pattie Maes
33. Marie-Chantal of Greece
34. Jeanine Pirro
35. Brad Pitt
36. Rebecca Romijn
37. Gavin Rossdale
38. Winona Ryder
39. Kristin Scott Thomas
40. Paul Sereno
41. Victoria Adams
42. Melanie Brown
43. Emma Bunton
44. Melanie Chisholm
45. Geri Halliwell
46. Gwen Stefani
47. Liv Tyler
48. Garrett Wang
49. Oprah Winfrey
50. Michelle Yeoh

26 CELEBRITIES WHO'VE MADE *PEOPLE* MAGAZINE'S ANNUAL LIST OF THE 50 MOST BEAUTIFUL PEOPLE IN THE WORLD MORE THAN ONCE

1. Tom Cruise (5)
2. Mel Gibson (5)
3. John F. Kennedy Jr. (5)
4. Michelle Pfeiffer (4)
5. Julia Roberts (4)
6. Halle Berry (4)
7. Antonio Banderas (3)
8. Kevin Costner (3)
9. Demi Moore (3)
10. Brad Pitt (3)
11. Claudia Schiffer (3)
12. Denzel Washington (3)
13. Juliette Binoche (2)
14. Toni Braxton (2)
15. George Clooney (2)
16. Cindy Crawford (2)
17. Whitney Houston (2)
18. Matt Lauer (2)
19. Jared Leto (2)
20. Daniel Day-Lewis (2)
21. Paul Newman (2)
22. Paulina Porizkova (2)
23. Jason Priestley (2)
24. Isabella Rossellini (2)
25. Winona Ryder (2)
26. Katarina Witt (2)

50 CELEBRITIES WHO MADE *PEOPLE* MAGAZINE'S 1998 LIST OF THE 50 MOST BEAUTIFUL PEOPLE IN THE WORLD

1. Leonardo DiCaprio
2. Prince William
3. Tony Blair
4. Erykah Badu
5. Helen Hunt
6. Matt Damon
7. Hunter Tylo
8. Bernard Parks
9. Gwyneth Paltrow
10. Julianna Margulies
11. Chris Carter
12. Brendan Fraser
13. Olivia Newton-John
14. Neve Campbell
15. Anne Bancroft
16. Will Smith
17. Sarah Michelle Gellar
18. Ilia Kulik
19. Celine Balitran
20. Andrea Bocelli
21. Tom Selleck
22. Palo Montalban
23. Anna Kournikova
24. Sandy Dalal
25. Angelina Jolie
26. Bai Ling
27. Ali Landry
28. Brian Mitchell
29. Stevie Nicks
30. Enrique Iglesias
31. Ann Curry
32. Dylan McDermott
33. Gloria Stuart
34. Catherine Zeta Jones
35. Danny Seo
36. Malia Jones
37. Alex Rodriguez
38. Rob Thomas
39. Chris Waddell
40. Arundhati Roy
41. Halle Berry
42. Cameron Diaz
43. James Van Der Beek
44. Julia Louis-Dreyfus
45. Troy Garrity
46. Calista Flockhart
47. Anne Heche
48. Blaine Trump
49. Bryan White
50. Cindy Margolis

1. Leonardo DiCaprio
2. Michael Owen
3. David Beckham
4. Ronan Keating
5. George Clooney
6. Adam Rickitt
7. Robbie Williams
8. Nick Carter
9. Brad Pitt
10. Matt Damon
11. Steve Houghton
12. Alan Shearer
13. Ewan McGregor
14. Ryan Giggs
15. Jamie Redknapp
16. Will Smith
17. Matthew Perry
18. David Ginola
19. Ross Kemp
20. Robson Green
21. Tom Cruise
22. Jon Bon Jovi
23. Mel Gibson
24. Marti Pellow
25. Steve Gately
26. Scott Robinson
27. Peter Andre
28. Teddy Sheringham
29. Will Mellor
30. Jesse Spencer
31. Adam Garcia
32. Paul Nicholls
33. David Seaman
34. Keanu reeves
35. Lee Brennan
36. Matt Marsden
37. David Duchovny
38. David Schwimmer
39. Prince William
40. George Michael
41. ABS
42. Johnny Vaughan
43. Noah Wyle
44. Jean-Claude Van Damme
45. Ally McCoist
46. Ian Wright
47. Mark Owen
48. Paul Ince
49. Kavana
50. Graeme Le Saux
51. Shane Lynch
52. Phil Neville
53. Eric Cantona
54. Gary Neville
55. Kevin Costner
56. Gary Barlow
57. Robert Carlyle
58. Stuart Wade
59. Ben Affleck
60. Damon Albam
61. Sean Bean
62. Skeet Ulrich
63. Howard Donald
64. Matt Le Blanc
65. Ben Freeman
66. Paul Gascoigne
67. Glenn Hoddle
68. Val Kilmer
69. Richard Gere
70. Christian Slater
71. Steve McManaman
72. Jason Orange
73. Hugo Speer
74. Tim Vincent
75. Prince Harry
76. Pierce Brosnan
77. William Baldwin
78. Mark Bannerman
79. Jamie Theakston
80. Antonhy Edwards
81. Will Carling
82. Jeremy Edwards
83. Patrick Swayze
84. Sting
85. Liam Gallagher
86. Paul Gross
87. Darren Day
88. David Coulthard
89. Sean Connery
90. Johnny Depp
91. Alessandro Del Piero
92. Nigel Benn
93. Ethan Hawke
94. Ben Unwin
95. Ruud Gullit
96. Richie
97. Harrison Ford
98. Kurt Russell
99. Puff Daddy
100. Tim Henman

78 FEMALE CELEBRITIES WHO CAN BE SEEN IN A STATE OF PARTIAL UNDRESS ON THE INTERNET

1. Bo Derek
2. Brigitte Nielsen
3. Brigitte Bardot
4. Cindy Crawford
5. Cybill Shepherd
6. Demi Moore
7. Elle McPherson
8. Farrah Fawcett
9. Gabrielle Anwar
10. Andie McDowell
11. Bridget Fonda
12. Catherine Bach
13. Claudia Schiffer
14. Darryl Hannah
15. Geri Halliwell
16. Gwyneth Paltrow
17. Helen Hunt
18. Ione Skye
19. Jane Fonda
20. Iman
21. Jamie Lee Curtis
22. Jennifer Aniston
23. Jenny McCarthy
24. Kate Moss
25. Kathleen Turner
26. Kelly McGillis
27. Madeline Stowe
28. Kim Basinger
29. Liv Tyler
30. Madonna
31. Mariel Hemingway
32. Meg Ryan
33. Mira Sorvino
34. Melanie Griffith
35. Michelle Pfeiffer
36. Mimi Rogers
37. Molly Ringwald
38. Morgan Fairchild
39. Natasha Henstridge
40. Nicole Kidman
41. Pamela Anderson Lee
42. Patsy Kensit
43. Phoebe Cates
44. Rachel Hunter
45. Sandra Bullock
46. Shannen Doherty
47. Susan Sarandon
48. Suzanne Somers
49. Tea Leoni
50. Teri Hatcher
51. Tori Amos
52. Vanna White
53. Tyra Banks
54. Vendela
55. Virginia Madsen
56. Gillian Anderson
57. Jennifer Jason Leigh
58. Amanda Donohoe
59. Anthea Turner
60. Dani Behr
61. Dannii Minogue
62. Kylie Minogue
63. Charlotte Rampling
64. Diane Keen
65. Emma Thompson
66. Elizabeth Hurley
67. Helen Mirren
68. Joanna Lumley
69. Lesley-Ann Down
70. Paula Yates
71. Stephanie Beacham
72. Vanessa Paradis
73. Steffi Graf
74. Caprice Bourret
75. Britt Ekland
76. Nastassja Kinski
77. Princess Stephanie of Monaco
78. Catherine Deneuve

15 MALE CELEBRITIES WHO CAN BE SEEN IN A STATE OF PARTIAL UNDRESS ON THE INTERNET

1. Arnold Schwarzenegger

2. Brad Pitt

3. Bruce Willis

4. Jason Priestley

5. Johnny Depp

6. Keanu Reeves

7. Jim Carrey

8. Jean-Claude Van Damme

9. Kevin Bacon

10. Rob Lowe

11. Sylvester Stallone

12. Sting

13. Patrick Swayze

14. Richard Gere

15. Mark Wahlberg

19 CELEBRITIES WHO HAVE BEEN AWARDED 'REAR OF THE YEAR'

1. Felicity Kendal
2. Lulu
3. Ulrika Jonsson
4. Elaine Pagie
5. Su Pollard
6. Marina Ogilvy
7. Anneka Rice
8. Barbara Windsor
9. Anita Dobson
10. Suzi Quatro
11. Melinda Messenger
12. Gary Barlow
13. Sarah Lancashire
14. Tracy Shaw
15. Richard Fairbrass
16. Lynsey de Paul
17. Michael Barrymore
18. Mandy Smith
19. James Crossley

Afterthought

―――― ―――― ―――― ―――― ―――― ―――― ――――

9 SEXUAL MYTHS

1. RICHARD GERE SHOVES GERBILS UP HIS JACKSEY!

Sadly, this is just not true. Notwithstanding the fact that you only have to mention the man's name for people to giggle about gerbils (and hamsters and guinea-pigs too, no doubt), this is a classic example of the old adage that a lie can be half the way round the world before the truth has got its boots on. The origins of this story bagan at a local radio station in Texas some 15 years ago. A local radio DJ was conducting a phone in when a listener rang in to say that Richard Gere (then just emerging as a major star) had a predilection for stuffing gerbils up his back passage. It was said as a joke and was received as such by the DJ who, nevertheless, enjoyed it so much that he repeated it quite a bit for the next few days. A listening DJ from Los Angeles was also quite taken by it and used it on his show back home. However, now it started to be taken seriously and the story spread, usually embellished in the retelling. The truth of the matter was that we all so desperately *wanted* it to be true that we eventually believed it to be true. Especially when Gere started getting all pally with the Dalai Lama and all that – it just seemed too good to be true that this seemingly saintly person had an unnatural, unhealthy interest in small furry creatures. I have a personal coda to add to this story. In 1995, Richard Gere was rumoured to be living on our Sussex seaside estate. Late one night I went past the door of the house where he was supposed to be staying and squeaked my heart out! No one emerged from the house – least of all a Hollywood superstar, and so I thought that was the end of it. But no! The following year, we happened to buy the very house in question, which was opposite the sea in a road named Tamarisk Way. The house itself, although beautiful in every way, had an extremely boring name and, bearing in mind its possible connection with Mr Gere and his alleged nocturnal pastimes (remember in 1996, before I knew better, I was still a believer in the myth), I thought about renaming the house 'Gerbils'. My wife (as wives do) knew better but sportingly suggested that we might look at a book about gerbils to find a more suitable name which wouldn't have to be explained to maiden aunts. And what do you think she discovered in this gerbil book? I'll tell you; there is apparently a breed of gerbil called the tamarisk gerbil. Spooky or what? Even so, it is still NOT TRUE!

2. CLARA BOW SLEPT WITH AN ENTIRE AMERICAN FOOTBALL TEAM ON THE SAME NIGHT!

Not so. Although Miss Bow bestowed her favours very liberally and included in her list of lovers many members of the USC team of 1927 so much so that their coach allegedly had to ban them from Clara's clutches – there is no evidence that she entertained them all together.

Catherine The Great supposedly died as a result of having sex with her horse. While the stories of her equine relationships are undoubtedly true, it is now thought that she actually died of a stroke.

3. ALL THE MEMBERS OF TAKE THAT WERE GAY!

This was a nasty rumour put about by jealous guys and bitchy non-fans. The truth is that when Nigel Martin-Smith, their manager, took them on, he decreed that they shouldn't have any *regular* girlfriends in case it upset their female fans. This was the same thinking which 30 years earlier had seen John Lennon hiding his wife Cynthia from the world.

4. MARIANNE FAITHFULL ONCE HAD A 'FOURSOME' WITH MICK JAGGER, KEITH RICHARDS AND A MARS BAR!

The truth of the story was that there was a drugs bust and Marianne was indeed unclothed. The rest is pure fantasy – denied by all those in attendance (though not the Mars Bar) – made up either by a journalist, a policeman or Peter Cook for *Private Eye* (as he himself later claimed). Along with the Richard Gere story, this is a story that everyone has always *wanted* to be true. Sadly it isn't.

5. PAUL SIMON AND ART GARFUNKEL WERE ONCE MARRIED!

Don't be silly. Even if they were gay, why get 'married'? For the record, they are both straight and married – though not to each other – and have children (Simon used to be married to Carrie Fisher). Duos are often prey to these sort of rumours – the same unfounded story was told of Marc Bolan and his percussionist, Mickey Finn.

6. THE PET SHOP BOYS NAMED THEMSELVES AFTER A BIZARRE SEXUAL PERVERSION!

This refers to Richard Gere (see above). Apparently, gerbils up the bum is something that extremely sick (and, let it be said, cruel) people do – although no one has ever stepped forward as a participant (well, certainly no gerbils have). Anyway, legend has it that The Pet Shop Boys' name alludes to this. In fact, the truth is much more mundane: Neil Tennant and Chris Lowe had some friends who worked in an Ealing pet shop.

7. WHEN MATA HARI WENT BEFORE THE FIRING SQUAD, SHE OPENED HER COAT TO REVEAL HER NAKED BODY – THUS RENDERING THE FIRING SQUAD INCAPABLE OF SHOOTING AT HER.

Not so.

8. DAVID GEFFEN AND KEANU REEVES WERE MARRIED IN A SECRET GAY WEDDING.

Nice try but for one thing. Keanu says that he's never even met Geffen – let alone *married* him.

9. CAPUCINE WAS A TRANSSEXUAL!

No, the actress wasn't but she was a lesbian which, for unenlightened Hollywood studio bosses, probably amounted to the same thing.

Bibliography

BIBLIOGRAPHY

Inevitably, a book like this draws on knowledge which has been accumulated over a period of years. Apart from very many newspaper and magazine articles, web sites on the internet and information from friends and colleagues, I read a great number of showbiz biographies/ autobiographies as background research. However, it is possible to specify some of the sources. The books below – all of which I would have no hesitation in recommending to anyone interested in further reading – were extremely helpful, either directly or indirectly, and I would like to express my sincere thanks to the authors responsible.

Misalliance by Edward Abelson (Macdonald, 1989)

How Do They Do It? edited by Reinhold Aman (Maledicta, 1983)

Who's Had Who by Simon Bell, Richard Curtis and Helen Fielding (Faber and Faber, 1987)

Entertainment Celebrity Register by Earl Blackwell (Visible Ink Press, 1992)

The Book of Royal Lists by Craig Brown and Lesley Cunliffe (Sphere Books, 1993)

The Naff Sex Guide by Doctor Kit Bryson, Selina Fitzherbert and Jean-Luc Legris (Arrow, 1994)

Sex Lives of The US Presidents by Nigel Cawthorne (Prion, 1996)

The Guinness Book of Classic British Television by Paul Cornell, Martin Day and Keith Topping (Guinness, 1993)

The Dirty Bits by Lesley Cunliffe, Craig Brown and Jon Connell (André Deutsch, 1981)

Sexual Trivia by Sarah Curtis (Ward Lock, 1986)

The Unofficial Book of Political Lists by Iain Dale (Robson Books, 1997)

Sex: An Encyclopedia for The Bewildered by K. S. Daly (Aurum, 1995)

Book of British Lists by Hunter Davies (Hamlyn Paperbacks 1980)

Bigger Book of British Lists by Hunter Davies (Hamlyn Paperbacks, 1992)

The English in Love: Passion Among The Elite by Anne De Courcy (Ebury Press, 1986)

TV Babylon by Paul Donnelley (Vista, 1997)

Sex Link by H Y Freedman (New English Library, 1978)

The Book Of Sex Lists compiled by Albert B. Gerber (W H Allen & Co, 1981)

An Unhurried view of Erotica by Ralph Ginzburg (Secker and Warburg, 1959)

Hollywood Lesbians by Boze Hadleigh (Barricade Books, 1994)

The Book Browsers Guide To Erotica by Roy Harley Lewis (David and Charles Ltd, 1981)

I'm Not One To Gossip But . . . by David Hartnell with Brian Williams (Futura, 1990)

The Bare Facts Video Guide by Craig Hosoda (The Bare Facts, 1994)

The Pan Dictionary of Famous Quotations compiled by Robin Hyman (Pan, 1989)

The Book of Erotic Failures by Peter Kinnell (Futura, 1984)

The Harlot by The Side of The Road, Forbidden Tales of The Bible by Jonathan Kirsch (Ballantine Books, 1997)

What Makes A Man G.I.B. (Good In Bed) by Wendy Leigh (Frederick Muller, 1980)

The American Sex Machines by Hoag Levins (Adams Media Corporation, 1996)

The Encyclopedia of Unusual Sex Practices by Brenda Love (Barricade Books, 1992)

The Celebrity Book of Lists by Ed Lucaire (Stein and Day, 1984)

The Celebrity Book of Super Lists by Ed Lucaire (Stein and Day, 1985)

Doing Rude Things, The History of The British Sex Film 1957-1981 by David McGillivray (Sun Tavern Fields, 1992)

Did She or Didn't She by Mart Martin (Carol Publishing, 1996)

Hollywood Lovers edited by Sheridan McCoid (Orion Media, 1997)

The Penguin Dictionary of Modern Humorous Quotations compiled by Fred Metcalf (Penguin, 1987)

The Juicy Parts by Jack Mingo (Berkley Publishing Group, 1996)

Weird Sex compiled by Steve Moore (John Brown Publishing, 1995)

Men on Sex by John Nicholson and Fiona Thompson (Vermilion, 1992)

The Bumper Book of Sex by Ray Nunn (Wolfe Publishing, 1967)

Cultural Icons by James Park (Bloomsbury, 1991)

Doktor Bey's Handbook of Strange Sex by Derek Pell (Avon, 1978)

20th Century Quotations compiled by Frank S. Pepper (Chaucer Press, 1985)

Working Girls; An Illustrated History Of the oldest Profession by Neil Phillip (Bloomsbury, 1991)

A Guide To America's Sex Laws by Richard A. Posner and Katherine B. Silbaugh (The University of Chicago, 1996)

Sex Trivia: The Bedside Guide by Nicholas Reed (Take That Books/MaxiMedia, 1995)

Lesbian Lists by Dell Richards (Alyson 1990)

The Guinness Book Of Almost Everything You Didn't Need to Know about Movies by Patrick Robertson (Guinness Superlatives Ltd, 1986)

Essential Film Guide by Simon Rose (HarperCollins, 1993)

The 1998 Entertainment Almanac edited by Beth Rowen (Straight Arrow, 1997)

The New Gay Book of Lists by Leigh W. Rutledge (Alyson, 1996)

Secret Lives by John Sachs and Piers Morgan (Blake Publishing, 1991)

Private Files of The Stars by John Sachs and Piers Morgan (Angus & Robertson, 1991)

Romantic Love and Society by Jacqueline Sarsby (Penguin, 1983)

The Professionals by Iain Scarlet (Sidgwick and Jackson, 1972)

The Female Member by Kit Schwartz (Robson Books, 1988)

The Celebrity Sex Register by Shirley Sealy (Fireside, 1982)

The Mammoth Book of Tasteless Lists by Karl Shaw (Robinson, 1998)

The Simons Book of Sexual Records by G.L. Simons (W.H. Allen, 1975)

The Illustrated Book of Sexual Records by G.L. Simons (Virgin Books, 1982)

The Encyclopaedia of Sexual Trivia by Doctor Robin Smith (Robson Books, 1990)

The Book of Aphrodisiacs by Doctor Raymond Stark, ND (Stein and Day, 1981)

A Pictorial History of Love by Paul Tabori (Spring, 1966)

The Visual Dictionary of Sex by Doctor Eric J. Trimmer (Pan, 1979)

The International Dictionary of 20th
Century Biography by Edward Vernoff
and Rima Shore (New American
Library, 1987)

The Secret Sex Lives of Famous
People by Irving Wallace, Amy
Wallace, David Wallechinsky and
Sylvia Wallace (Cresset, 1993).

The Book of Lists by David
Wallechinsky, Irving Wallace and Amy
Wallace (Corgi, 1977)

The Book of Lists 2 by David
Wallechinsky, Irving Wallace and Amy
Wallace (Elm Tree Books/ Hamish
Hamilton, 1980)

The Book of Lists 3 by David
Wallechinsky, Irving Wallace and Amy
Wallace (Corgi, 1984)

The Book of Lists: The 90s Edition by
David Wallechinsky and Amy Wallace
(Aurum Press, 1994)

Hotlips by Noelle Walsh (Ebury Press,
1985)

Looney Sex Laws by Robert Wayne
Pelton (Walker, 1992)

Bluff Your Way in Sex by Tim Webb
and Sarah Brewer (Ravette, 1987)

Dictionary of Erotic Literature by H.E.
Wedeck (Peter Owen, 1962)

The Complete Book of Sexual Trivia
by Leslee Welch (Carol Publishing,
1992)

Sex Facts: A Handbook For The
Carnally Curious by Leslee Welch
(Carol Publishing, 1995)

Sex and Sexuality A Thematic
Dictionary of Quotations (Cassell,
1993)

The 1998 People Weekly
Entertainment Almanac (People
Books, 1997)

Sexual Trivia (The Dinner Party
Edition) (Paul Lamond Games Ltd.)

The First Time by Karl Fleming and
Anne Taylor Fleming (Simon &
Schuster, 1975)

Please address orders to:

Littlehampton Book Services
14 Eldon Way
Lineside Estate
Littlehampton
West Sussex
BN17 7HE
Tel: 01903 721596
Fax: 01903 730914
Email: 100067.163@compuserve.com

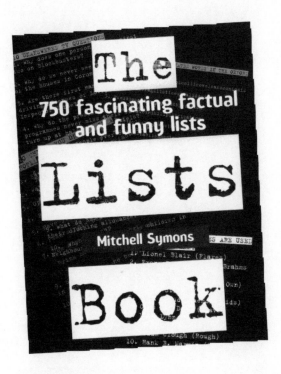

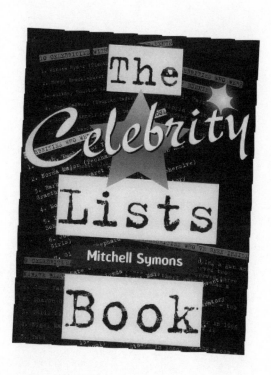

The Lists Book
Mitchell Symons
ISBN 0 233 99413 0
£7.99

The Celebrity Lists Books
Mitchell Symons
ISBN 0 233 99111 5
£7.99